A Discipleship House Study Guide

The Great Quest

by Penn Clark

Adventures in Guidance, Vision, and Hearing the Voice of God

THE GREAT QUEST

Adventures in Guidance, Vision, and Hearing the Voice of God

2021 © Copyright by Penn Clark
Published by Wordsmith Publishing of Penn Yan, New York

All rights reserved. This book or parts thereof may not be reproduced in any form, except for brief quotations in reviews, without the express permission of the publisher. This material and material published on the related web pages listed herein are the creative property of Penn Clark and may not be reproduced for distribution in any form. However, they may be used for personal edification or for small group study without prior permission.

Both Discipleship House and Wordsmith Publishing are ministries of WellSpring Fellowship, which is a nonprofit 501 C3. Our office address is 217 W. Main St., Penn Yan, New York 14527. For current contact information and the latest editions of Wordsmith Study Guides, go to our website (www.pennclark.net).

The mission of Wordsmith Publishing is to provide teaching and training materials, using all forms of media, in order to advance the Kingdom of God both here and overseas. It is our desire to help more believers become committed disciples of the living Christ.

Scripture quotations are taken from the New King James Version®. Copyright © 1982 by Thomas Nelson, Inc. Used by permission. All rights reserved.

Scripture quotations marked (KJV) are taken from the *Holy Bible*, King James Version, Cambridge, 1769, public domain.

Scripture quotations marked (AMP) are taken from the Amplified Bible, Copyright © 2015 by The Lockman Foundation. Used by permission.

Scripture quotations marked (ASV) are taken from the American Standard Version, 1901, public domain.

Scripture quotations marked (BBE) are taken from the 1949/1964 BIBLE IN BASIC ENGLISH, public domain.

Scripture quotations marked (GNT) are from the Good News Translation in Today's English Version- Second Edition Copyright © 1992 by American Bible Society. Used by Permission.

Scripture quotations marked (TLB) are taken from *The Living Bible* copyright © 1971. Used by permission of Tyndale House Publishers, Inc., Carol Stream, Illinois 60188. All rights reserved.

Scripture quotations marked (CEV) are taken from the Contemporary English Version Copyright © 1991, 1992, 1995 by the American Bible Society. Used by permission.

Scripture quotations marked (GWT) are taken from GOD'S WORD®, © 1995 God's Word to the Nations. Used by permission of Baker Publishing Group.

Scripture quotations marked (MSG) are taken from *THE MESSAGE*, copyright © 1993, 2002, 2018 by Eugene H. Peterson. Used by permission of NavPress. All rights reserved. Represented by Tyndale House Publishers, a Division of Tyndale House Ministries.

Scripture quotations marked (NCV) are taken from the New Century Version®. Copyright © 2005 by Thomas Nelson. Used by permission. All rights reserved.

Scripture quotations marked (NIV) are taken from the Holy Bible, New International Version®, NIV®. Copyright © 1973, 1978, 1984, 2011 by Biblica, Inc.™

Scripture quotations marked (NIrV) are taken from the Holy Bible, New International Reader's Version®, NIrV® Copyright © 1995, 1996, 1998, 2014 by Biblica, Inc.™ Used by permission of Zondervan. All rights reserved worldwide. www.zondervan.com The "NIrV" and "New International Reader's Version" are trademarks registered in the United States Patent and Trademark Office by Biblica, Inc.™

Scripture quotations marked (NLT) are taken from the Holy Bible, New Living Translation, copyright ©1996, 2004, 2015 by Tyndale House Foundation. Used by permission of Tyndale House Publishers, a Division of Tyndale House Ministries, Carol Stream, Illinois 60188. All rights reserved.

Scripture quotations marked (TPT) are taken from The Passion Translation®. Copyright © 2017, 2018 by Passion & Fire Ministries, Inc. Used by permission. All rights reserved. ThePassionTranslation.com.

Scripture quotations marked (WEB) are taken from The World English Bible (WEB): World English Bible, public domain.

Bold type in Scripture quotations has been added by the author for emphasis.

"Part Two: Getting a Glimpse" and "Part Five: Asking, Seeking, and Knocking" were taken in part from *The Day* © 2019. It was written by Penn Clark and published by Wordsmith Publishing. Used by permission of the author.

"Part Three: God's Ultimate and Immediate Will" was taken in part from *Cultivating Your Call* © 2014. It was written by Penn Clark and published by Wordsmith Publishing. Used by permission of the author.

"Part Ten: Guidelines to Guidance" was taken in part from *Cultivating Your Call* © 2014 and *A Place for Prophecy* © 2019. Both books were written by Penn Clark and published by Wordsmith Publishing. Used by permission of the author.

Edited by Abbie and Edie Mourey (www.furrowpress.com).

Special thanks for their help with this project go to Heather Clark, Norman Morrison, Marta Marino, and Ruth Sommers.

The cover photo was taken by the author. The photos of Penn were taken by Riley Helmuth at High Braise Retreat, Redfield, New York.

Ask us about a special bulk rate anytime you order any Wordsmith publications for small group studies and discipleship groups.

ISBN-13: 978-1-947472-21-1 (Print)

ISBN: 978-1-947472-22-8 (eBook)

Look for this book and others in this series on our on-line store at www.wordsmith-py.com

ABOUT PENN CLARK

Penn and Heather Clark left their native Canada with a missionary visa to help start a church in northern New York, where they pastored for more than twenty-one years. Penn formed Word of Grace Network, an apostolic fellowship of like-minded ministers committed to world missions, raising up the next generation of leaders, and equipping others to advance the Kingdom of God.

The Lord has sent Penn to some of the neediest places on Earth, where he has taught and trained leaders, helped start churches, and enabled the poor to help themselves. Penn's ministry is based in Penn Yan, New York, at WellSpring Fellowship, a church he helped start in the beautiful Finger Lakes region.

To learn more about Penn, go to www.pennclark.net or at www.pennclark.study

There are many different kinds of smiths in the world. There are blacksmiths, tinsmiths, and goldsmiths, but what vocation can be higher than to be able to spend one's life working with words? Words can be wrought in such a way as to change an individual's life. Consider the enormous privilege of spending a lifetime handling God's Word, which transforms and enriches lives. Furthermore, it inspires us to love God for all eternity. What can be more valuable than that which has been wrought by God's Word?

Wordsmith Study Guides and Booklets were originally written for those in our local church who were in leadership or were preparing for the ministry. In time, I began to print them in a newsletter format, sending them out to various church leaders and those who prayed for my ministry. When the Internet became available, I decided it would be more expedient to publish Wordsmith online. Over the years, this has been a proven way to invest in the lives of those who are in ministry or are being trained for it.

TABLE OF CONTENTS

INTRODUCTION: THE GREAT QUESTS IN LIFE 8

PART ONE: THE MAPMAKER 11

PART TWO: GETTING A GLIMPSE 18

PART THREE: GOD'S ULTIMATE AND IMMEDIATE WILL 26

PART FOUR: DISCERNING THE WILL OF GOD 33

PART FIVE: ASKING, SEEKING, AND KNOCKING 43

PART SIX: FIGHTING FOR THE WILL OF GOD 58

PART SEVEN: DISCERNING GOD'S VOICE 62

PART EIGHT: CULTIVATING A HEARING HEART 73

PART NINE: GUIDELINES TO GUIDANCE 80

PART TEN: QUESTIONS AND ANSWERS 93

REFERENCE NOTES 111

ADDENDUM ONE: PRAYERS AND PROMISES FOR GUIDANCE 112

ADDENDUM TWO: PROMISES THAT BUILD ASSURANCE 115

ADDENDUM THREE: PROMISES AND PRINCIPLES OF GUIDANCE 117

ADDENDUM FOUR: BOOKS I RECOMMEND 119

INTRODUCTION: THE GREAT QUESTS IN LIFE

Like many others, I enjoy a good quest. After all, we all need something to shoot for, and the more challenging the better. The more unusual something is, the more we want to go for it and be the first in line to try it. We also desire to leave our mark, carve our niche, or stand out from the crowd.

Most of the great quests, like climbing each of the fourteen highest peaks in the world, have already been achieved. In fact, so many people have made Mount Everest their great quest that it has created traffic jams on the mountain. Then, there are the already realized solo quests like walking across the Arctic, circumnavigating the globe in a hot air balloon, or exploring the deepest parts of the ocean in a submarine. Some quests are far out like the man who wanted to free fall from the edge of space.

One jaw-dropping quest that caught my eye recently was the young guy who climbed El Capitan without a safety rope. Another incredible quest included a person jumping from a plane without a parachute and landing in a giant net. Not too long ago, I read an article about an elderly Frenchman trying to float across the Atlantic Ocean in a barrel that he built for that purpose.

Quests come in all shapes and sizes. Not all of these quests require physical skills. Some are of the sedentary variety, such as writing a bestselling novel or solving a medical mystery. Some quests are financial, some are educational, and others can be social. All of these quests can be as difficult as climbing Everest. Additionally, there is no end to the inventions people come up with, the schemes, scams, and the wacky stuff they hope will put them in the pages of *The Guinness Book of World Records* or on some television show like *Shark Tank*.

There are some quests that are spiritual in nature. Evangelist Dwight L. Moody has been often quoted as saying: "The world has yet to see what God can do with a man fully consecrated to Him. By God's help, I aim to be that man."[1]

Now, that is one great quest!

People often define their purpose by what they *do*, as opposed to who they will *be*. Ask someone what their vision is, and they will likely start by reciting their to-do list. In this Study Guide, I want to set in front of you some great quests that are worth giving ourselves to. They will always hold our interest and will change our lives and the lives of others. These great quests will provide all the adventure we could ever want.

As a young man, Jim Elliot became one of the most influential American missionaries. He died in 1958 at the hands of a primitive tribe that he was trying to reach with the gospel. His death was not in vain. His ministry inspired an entire generation to give their all for the Lord. Several books and movies have been made about his life. Long before anyone had heard of Jim, he started his

---

Ask someone what their vision is, and they will likely start by reciting their to-do list.

own great quest by deeply surrendering his life to God and choosing God's will above his own. Here are lines taken from his diary, written when he was only twenty-five years old:

> In my own experience, I have found that the most extravagant dreams of boyhood could not surpass the great experience of being in the will of God. And I believe that nothing could be better. This is not to say that I do not want other things, and other ways of living, and other places to see, but in my right mind, I know that my hopes and plans for myself could not be better than what He has arranged. Thus, may we all find it and know the truth of the Word of God, which says, "He will be our guide unto death."[2]

One of the great quests I embarked on as a young disciple turned into a lifelong pursuit. When I first began to study the Bible for myself, I came to believe that God wrote a purpose for my life before I was created and that He kept it reserved in a book in heaven until I came to be. I believe the same is true about you. Gradually, through our cooperation and persistence, God reveals what He planned for us. This is what we call vision. I have had many moments where the eyes of my heart were opened to perceive the will of God for my life. I believe that we do not just stumble upon our purpose. Instead, we need to pray it into existence, bringing the will of God from heaven to the earth just as Jesus taught us to pray. Nothing this important should ever be left to chance or circumstance.

Included in pursuit of this great quest has been the need to hear God's voice. This has not only helped me prioritize my life around what His priorities are, as revealed in His Word, but has helped me to come into my purpose. Learning to hear His voice has been essential in helping me take the immediate steps needed to stand in the will of God in every area of my life. As my wife, Heather, and I have looked back on our lives, we see how God drafted our story.

This reflection has brought order and symmetry to our lives along with a deep satisfaction that comes from trusting God, who holds the future in His hands. While I am still learning how to find God's will for my life, what I have learned over the past forty plus years I have tried to put into this Study Guide. I have tried to keep things as simple and childlike as possible. There are things that are too high for me, things I don't understand, such as all the ins and outs of Calvinism versus Arminianism. There are also things that don't interest me, like aspects of predestination and arguments about freewill. You cannot draw me into an argument along these lines because they do not hold my interest. I prefer to keep things simple, straightforward, and scriptural.

This book contains my vision of how to find and fight for the will of God. This has kept my interest and keeps me focused on what is important. I want to encourage you to be childlike rather than living in hesitancy and doubt about things that are hard to understand. I can enjoy a coffee without having to understand everything about coffee. The same is true about the will of God.

> I prefer to keep things simple, straightforward, and scriptural.

There is plenty I do not understand, but what I do grasp of His will is enough to allow me to enjoy the journey. It is my hope that this Study Guide will inspire you in your own quest to know God's will for your life. I hope you come to know the peace of surrender and the adventure of following the One who has already written a book about your life.

With every blessing, Penn

PART ONE: THE MAPMAKER

Once while on a personal retreat, seeking the Lord for direction, I came across an old copy of a modern English Bible called *The Way*. On the back cover was a picture of a compass and the text of Jeremiah 10:23:

> *"O Lord, I know it is not within the power of man to map his life or plan his course—so you correct me, Lord; but please be gentle. Don't do it in your anger or I will die."*

This verse put into words why I was on that trip in the first place. I had come to the end of myself. Once again, I realized that I was not wise enough to decide what course my life needed to take. I longed for God to show me His will, so I could realign my life with it. I didn't want Him to be angry with me for getting off track or asking for more again; so like Jeremiah, I asked for His patience. I also took comfort in James 1:5, as I often do, where He promised to give an abundance of perspective (wisdom) without finding fault. When we admit that we need help, He won't be standing over us, tapping His toe and shaking His finger, saying, "You made this mess, now get yourself out of it!" Instead, He promises to give us all the perspective we need to be able to move on from the messes we get ourselves into.

THE BOOK OF DAYS

The Lord is an author. He delights in writing books. David had a revelation that God wrote books about him:

> *You number my wanderings; put my tears into Your bottle; are they not in Your book?* (Psalm 56:8)

He saw that God not only keeps track of our journeys, like a mapmaker, but He already laid out everything about us ahead of time. David, as a young prophet, caught a revelation that all his days were prerecorded in a book before he was born:

> *Your eyes saw my substance, being yet unformed. And in Your book they all were written, the days fashioned for me, when as yet there were none of them. How precious also are Your thoughts to me, O God! How great is the sum of them! If I should count them, they would be more in number than the sand; when I awake, I am still with You.* (Psalm 139:16-18)

For clarity, here are the same verses taken from Today's Living Bible:

> *You watched me as I was being formed in utter seclusion, as I was woven together in the dark of the womb. You saw me before I was born. Every day of my life was recorded in your book. Every moment was laid out*

David, as a young prophet, caught a revelation that all his days were prerecorded in a book before he was born.

before a single day had passed. How precious are your thoughts about me, O God! They are innumerable! (Psalm 139:15-17)

It was revealed to David that God's thoughts about him were more numerous than the grains of sand on an ocean shore. These were not just passing thoughts, but actual predestined plans and purposes. David said that His plans were more numerous than the sand. How would you like to count a bucketful of sand? If you tried to count just a handful of sand, you wouldn't be able to do it! David understood that God's plans and intentions for his life were as innumerable as the sand! I wonder if he had this revelation on a desert, where he could see nothing but sand in every direction.

I have met many believers who are self-willed and carnally minded, living cobbled up lives while believing they are in the will of God. Their lives have no peace, no pattern, and no evidence of planning. They go from fruitlessness to frivolity, wrongfully concluding that they are being led by the Lord. Then, they blame God for all their failed plans—plans which He could never have written because He is not the author of confusion (1 Corinthians 14:33).

IT'S ALL IN THE ABIDING

If your life is boring, lifeless, empty, confusing, fruitless, aimless, and broken, it is likely that you are not living out of what God has planned for your life. You are living out of your own plans and purposes. Jesus talked about a level of fruitfulness that occurs in our lives as we learn to abide in Him:

If you abide in Me, and My words abide in you, you will ask what you desire, and it shall be done for you. By this My Father is glorified, that you bear much fruit; so you will be My disciples. (John 15:7-8)

The more we abide in the Lord and in His Word, our minds and motives become one with His. When this happens, He can trust us to do so much more because we tend to be more in sync with His will. Much more can be accomplished through us as a result. It's all in the abiding. Conversely, the more self-willed we are, the less we experience the wonder of His will at work in our lives.

THE ARCHITECT

God is the Master Planner, who thinks like an architect, laying things out in advance with cause, effect, order, and balance. He has the end in mind right from the beginning and does what it takes to make things work while factoring in our own choices. When we look back on His leading, we can see how it all makes sense. We find that our lives are progressive, not random or scattered with abrupt turns and dead ends. Our lives should evidence one thing leading to another because it was planned out by the greatest Mind in the universe. This is one reason why He speaks with such authority in Scripture:

I am God, and there is none else; I am God, and there is none like me, declaring the end from the beginning, and from ancient times the things that are not yet done, saying, My counsel shall stand, and I will do all my pleasure. (Isaiah 46:9-10)

He can do this because He wrote everything out before it was.

The Lord of hosts has sworn, saying, "Surely, as I have planned, so it shall come to pass, and as I have purposed, so it shall stand." (Isaiah 14:24)

I believe that, if we will wait upon Him, allowing our desires and motives to get in sync with His, more of His will can be realized. Far too often, however, we do our own thing. We forfeit what He planned and settle for the best we can come up with on our own. We may even just do what our circumstances throw our way.

For I know the plans I have for you, says the Lord. They are plans for good and not for evil, to give you a future and a hope. (Jeremiah 29:11 TLB)

I believe the Lord wrote a plan for our lives according to what brought Him the most amount of pleasure. We will find our purpose by seeking what brings Him pleasure. Our own pleasure in life is indelibly linked to His.

Our own pleasure in life is indelibly linked to His.

JESUS' LIFE WAS PREORDAINED

The only place we need to look for evidence of God's preordained plan for our lives is Jesus' life. There are almost fifty prophecies detailing what He would do and how He would live. Events of His life had been prewritten, including His birth, His ministry, His death, and His second coming. As He and His earthly parents sought to please His heavenly Father, submitting to God the Father's will, the Father's will began to manifest in Jesus' life on Earth. The same thing happens for us today.

What the Old Testament prophets foretold included everything from what Jesus would eat to His riding on a baby donkey. They contained details like where He would be born and grow up and to where He would flee. They also contained much about who He would be and what He would do. Sometimes, they included what He would teach and how He would say it.

All the prophecies pertaining to Jesus came to pass with astonishing accuracy. This was not because He was the Son of God. This occurred because Jesus was called according to His purpose and beloved. The fact that you exist is all the proof you need to know that God has written a plan of your life before you were on Earth.

Jesus knew His purpose was preordained. He even read His God-given purpose, written hundreds of years before, as He stood before His home congregation at Nazareth, reading from Isaiah's scroll, *"The Spirit of the Lord is upon me, because God has anointed me to...."* The word *anointed* used here also means *appointed or mandated* (see Luke 4:18-19).

JUDAS'S LIFE WAS ALSO PREORDAINED

Someone might say, "Well, that only happened because He was the Son of God. It does not mean it will happen for others." Well, it happened for Judas:

And in those days Peter stood up in the midst of the disciples (altogether the number of names was about a hundred and twenty), and said, "Men and brethren, this Scripture had to be fulfilled, which the Holy Spirit spoke before by the mouth of David concerning Judas, who became a guide to those who arrested Jesus; for he was numbered with us and obtained a part in this ministry." (Now this man purchased a field with the wages of iniquity; and falling headlong, he burst open in the middle and all his entrails gushed out. And it became known to all those dwelling in Jerusalem; so that field is called in their own language, Akel Dama, that is, Field of Blood.) "For it is written in the Book of Psalms: 'Let his dwelling place be desolate, and let no one live in it'; and, 'Let another take his office.'" (Acts 1:15-20)

If this happened for Judas, we can expect that our lives are preordered by God. Do you believe that?

> The first Christians believed that their lives and purposes were predetermined by God.

The first Christians believed that their lives and purposes were predetermined by God:

*For in this city both Herod and Pontius Pilate actually met together with the Gentiles and the people of Israel against your holy servant Jesus, whom you anointed, to do all that your hand and your will had **predetermined** to take place.* (Acts 4:27-28 ISV)

PAUL'S UNDERSTANDING OF OUR PREORDAINED PURPOSE

The apostle Paul wrote quite a bit about his understanding of God's preordained will. He also prayed for the Ephesians that the eyes of their understanding would be opened in such a way that they would also see what God saw for them:

Blessed be the God and Father of our Lord Jesus Christ, who has blessed us with every spiritual blessing in the heavenly places in Christ, just as He chose us in Him before the foundation of the world, that we should be holy and without blame before Him in love, having predestined us to adoption as sons by Jesus Christ to Himself, according to the good pleasure of His will, to the praise of the glory of His grace, by which He made us accepted in the Beloved. (Ephesians 1:3-6)

He went on to write how God's will, purpose, and good pleasure were one and the same:

Having made known to us the mystery of His will, according to His good pleasure which He purposed in Himself. (1:9)

Paul told them that our purpose was predestined according to God's purpose:

In Him also we have obtained an inheritance, being predestined according to the purpose of Him who works all things according to the counsel of His will. (v. 11)

Therefore I also, after I heard of your faith in the Lord Jesus and your love for all the saints, do not cease to give thanks for you, making mention of you in my prayers: that the God of our Lord Jesus Christ, the Father of glory, may give to you the spirit of wisdom and revelation in the knowledge of Him the eyes of your understanding being enlightened; that you may know what is the hope of His calling, what are the riches of the glory of His inheritance in the saints, and what is the exceeding greatness of His power toward us who believe, according to the working of His mighty power. He also said that God had good works hidden in each day for us to discover and to walk out: For by grace you have been saved through faith, and that not of yourselves; it is the gift of God, not of works, lest anyone should boast. For we are His workmanship, created in Christ Jesus for good works, which God prepared beforehand that we should walk in them. (2:8-10)

As we study the verses above, we see we were not saved *by* our good works, but we are saved *for* good works. While we can't ever be good enough or do enough good to get God to save us, once we are saved, He expects us to do good works. He did not intend for us to sit on the sidelines. God has preordained, or prewritten, various good works for us to discover in life. It is our responsibility to find out what these are and walk them out. Our fulfillment lies both in the seeking and the finding. If we are not fulfilled at a heart level, perhaps we are not doing what we have been created to do.

Our book, which He has written before we were, contains His will for our lives. I personally believe that, if we were to die right now and go to heaven, we could see an actual book with our name on it that contains His will for our lives. This would explain why Jesus said we must pray that His will which is in heaven be done in the earth (Matthew 6:10). Our purposes are not floating around up there; I believe they are contained in books.

I also believe the unfolding of this plan is not automatic or guaranteed. We must want it. We must pray that His will happens. In fact, we must humbly insist upon it. Many believers do not do this, so they live unfulfilled, cobbled up lives, thinking somehow whatever happens to them must be the will of God.

> **Our purpose should have a progression to it, which unfolds in an orderly way as if it were written by a master planner or an incredible author.**

To look at some people's meanderings though, you would think their lives were written by a drunken sailor. Some people's lives are so disorganized and disorderly that God could not have written a plan like that, because He is not the author of confusion. He is the author of peace and order (1 Corinthians 14:33). Our purpose should have a progression to it, which unfolds in an orderly way as if it were written by a master planner or an incredible author. If you lack vision for the coming year or your original vision needs to be refreshed, this study will help you begin to seek the Lord about your purpose.

GETTING MORE PURPLE IN OUR LIVES

As a young disciple, I could not get my head around the idea that God had a purpose for my life. I couldn't comprehend that this purpose was predestined before I was, and wasn't something that was changed because of my performance. The fact that He allows me to make my own decisions along the way was astounding to me.

One day, I asked the Lord to help me understand these complicated concepts. He showed me a simple picture to help me grasp the complex concept of predestination. I saw a blue ribbon draped across a map with a thumbtack stuck in the ribbon's beginning. This represented the day I was conceived in my mother's womb. The blue ribbon coursed through my life and circumstances, winding through geographic locations, crossing other people's lives, and meandering through various events. Then, when the thumbtack was placed at the end of the blue ribbon, that was the end of my life on Earth. I pictured this as God's will for my life, which He wrote for me before I ever was. He wrote my life's story without prejudice toward me or based upon my performance as a Christian now. He didn't craft failure and dishonor. He wrote something wonderful. He wrote my story in a book, put my name on it, and closed it until the day of my birth.

Then, I saw another ribbon, a red one. It was similarly placed on the map with a tack at its start. It represented my will. Sometimes, the blue and red ribbon traveled together, making it seem as if there were a purple ribbon on the map. Other times, the ribbons would go off in separate directions and from time to time cross back over each other. Sometimes, the blue and red ribbons seemed close to each other or appeared to run parallel.

I believe God wrote my life before I ever was created or born. I have made choices and mapped my own course by my choices or my will. Sometimes, my will has slipped into God's Will. Other times, they parallel, and sometimes, they have been far apart. I believe you can write your own book. You can be anything or do anything; however, you will never be satisfied unless you are aligned with what He designed for you to do and who He wants you to be. You can choose which life you would rather have: the one He wrote for you or the one you make up yourself. He hopes you choose His.

> **I believe God wrote my life before I ever was created or born.**

I want more purple in my life, don't you? You know who gets the purple, don't you? Those who insist upon having what He wrote for them. Those who say, "I want Your will for my life. I know I can have my will. I have tasted that, now I am asking for what You have planned for my life. Choose for me, oh God. I want what is in Your book for my life."

He says, "That's what I want also. If you will let Me, I will reveal My plans for your life."

It takes time to bring about such an alignment; it takes moving in obedience and sorting out your motives through prayer. You must be insistent. You cannot simply coast along and happen to get into the will of God.

I feel that for a large part of my life now I have been in the will of God. There is so much in my life that I am satisfied with. I know God is using me, and I have sensed His pleasure in what I am doing right now. This does not ensure that there will never be bad days. Look at Joseph. Watch Jesus. His life was planned up to the second, and He submitted completely to the will of His Father. Jesus' heart lived in the statement, "I will always say and do those things that please My Father." Yet He suffered in this life. Joseph had doors opened that no man could close. He also had doors closed that no man could open. Some of those doors opened to a dry well, and others revealed prison cells. In other words, not all of our experiences are good, but they eventually lead to God's main purpose for us and are part of His plan for us.

ASSIGNMENT

Take time to read Psalm 41:9; Psalm 109; Zechariah 11:12-13; and Acts 1:16, looking for the evidence that Judas's life was preordained. It may be strange to say this, but the fact is Judas had a purpose.

Jesus knew His purpose. He knew what He was ordained to do. He even read His God-given purpose to the congregation in Nazareth in Luke 4:18-19, where He said,

"The Spirit of the Lord is upon me, because God has anointed me to...."

The word *anointed* used here also means *appointed* or *mandated*. What have you been appointed to do? Can you write it out in specific terms, using concise language? Why don't you use this for an opening line and fill in the rest—write, *"The Spirit of the Lord is upon [your name], because He has anointed me to _____."*

What are you appointed to do? Write it out in specific terms, using concise language that would help you remember it.

What have you been appointed to do?

PART TWO: GETTING A GLIMPSE

Whenever we get a glimpse of what God has purposed for our lives, it is called vision. With the eyes of our hearts, we are allowed a peek at our purpose. God wants us to see it. In fact, it is in our best interest for Him to show us. We always do better after we see part of our purpose. There are several scriptures that indicate God's willingness to show us, in advance, what He has written for us:

> *"Remember the former things of old, for I am God, and there is no other; I am God, and there is none like Me, declaring the end from the beginning, and from ancient times things that are not yet done, saying, 'My counsel shall stand, and I will do all My pleasure,' calling a bird of prey from the east, the man who executes My counsel, from a far country. Indeed I have spoken it; I will also bring it to pass. I have purposed it; I will also do it."* (Isaiah 46:9-11)

> *"Thus says the Lord, The Holy One of Israel, and his Maker: 'Ask Me of things to come concerning My sons; And concerning the work of My hands, you command Me.'"* (Isaiah 45:11)

> *"However, when He, the Spirit of truth, has come, He will guide you into all truth; for He will not speak on His own authority, but whatever He hears He will speak; and He will tell you things to come."* (John 16:13)

We are allowed a peek at our purpose.

THE DANGER OF NOT HAVING A PROGRESSIVE VISION

When I said that it is in our best interest to have an ongoing vision, it is because He knows that without a vision, we will perish:

> *Where there is no vision, the people perish; but blessed are those who keep the law.* (Proverbs 29:18)

The New King James Version *margin notes read:* "*Where there is no prophetic vision....*"

The word *perish* means *"to be unruly"* or *"to become lawless."* Perhaps this is why the other half of the Proverb says, *"but blessed are those who keep the law."*

Other translations shed more light on this verse:

"Where there is no revelation the people cast off restraint...." (NIV)

"Where there is no clear prophetic vision, people quickly wander astray." (TPT)

"Without prophetic vision people run wild...." (GWT)

Without a progressive vision we dwell precariously. We are to live with certainty not in a precarious manner, relying on "chance" to guide us.

SOLOMON DID NOT HAVE A PROGRESSIVE VISION

The idea of dwelling precariously is best illustrated by the life of Solomon, who had originally been given vision to build the temple of God. Once that vision was completed, he did not press in for more vision. In time, he lost all restraint and began living contrary to the will of God.

From his own words in Ecclesiastes, we can see where he became self-indulgent, focusing upon his desires. He began to collect wealth, wives, and horses, all of which the Lord had personally warned him against doing. He gave himself to every excessive appetite, which the enemy used to bring him down. How far did he fall? The Lord used Solomon to build His temple, oversee the arrangement of priestly ministry, and write Scripture. Solomon also had two open visitations from the Lord. Yet, Solomon gave himself over to Ashtoreth, which was the Canaanite fertility goddess, whose worship not only involved sexual rites but also astrology. She was the female counterpart to Baal. Numerous clay plaques depicting naked female images have been found in Palestine, home of the Canaanites. As a part of these rituals, women were obliged to sacrifice their chastity.

None of this satisfied Solomon's heart's desires, though, and eventually these things led him astray. Many pastors and business leaders become like Solomon. After they reach a certain level of success in their work or ministry, they do not seek for more vision and turn to sexually or monetarily immoral practices, desperately searching for meaning. I call this the *Solomon Syndrome*. We will never be satisfied unless we are doing what God created us to do by actively seeking after His will for the various stages of our lives.

> **We will never be satisfied unless we are doing what God created us to do.**

EVIDENCES OF A LACK OF VISION

Here is a list of things I have experienced whenever I have lost sight of the vision God has given me:

1. A greater desire for entertainment and reverting to the former pleasures I enjoyed before I knew the Lord
2. An increase in sexual appetites
3. A decrease in spiritual motivation
4. Slow to resist temptation and sin
5. An increase of criticism (and fault-finding) of myself and of others
6. A growing desire for quick, spiritual pick-me-ups
7. Increased time and energy spent on non-eternal interests

8. A serious loss of priorities

9. Increased shows of temper, frustration, and melancholy

10. A sense of being under the constant disapproving gaze of God

The apostle Paul kept his eye on a heavenly vision, which gave him the discipline needed to keep his flesh under control. His vision also enabled him to endure whatever hardships that came his way. It was this vision that helped him run the race of faith:

Do you not know that those who run in a race all run, but one receives the prize? Run in such a way that you may obtain it. And everyone who competes for the prize is temperate in all things. Now they do it to obtain a perishable crown, but we for an imperishable crown. Therefore I run thus: not with uncertainty. Thus I fight: not as one who beats the air. But I discipline my body and bring it into subjection, lest, when I have preached to others, I myself should become disqualified. (1 Corinthians 9:24-27)

If you have accomplished anything in this life, you soon realize how little there is down here that holds your interest. Whether your goal is to become a millionaire or a minister, you will soon be disappointed once you arrive at your goal because it will not satisfy you the way you thought it would. We need more eternal goals.

I am trying to prioritize my life around seeking the Lord and finding more of His purpose to pursue. Having an eternal vision is the only vision that will satisfy us.

WITHOUT A VISION, WE WILL MAKE UP OUR OWN

When there is no vision from God, people tend to make up their own. Sometimes, they even call it God's will, not realizing their own hearts are capable of and have created their own vision.

"Thus says the Lord of hosts: 'Do not listen to the words of the prophets who prophesy to you. They make you worthless; they speak a vision of their own heart, not from the mouth of the Lord.'" (Jeremiah 23:16)

In the mid-1500s, explorer Martin Frobisher entered the Arctic region of northern Canada looking for the Northwest Passage. He was the first European man to enter the Hudson Strait and Frobisher Bay, which was later named after him. He did not find the elusive Northwest Passage, but he did find lots of ore flecked with gold. He was so excited by this discovery that he dumped much of the provisions needed to get his crew safely back to England. He filled every inch of the storage area of his ship with tons of ore and headed for home as quickly as he could, barely making it. His hasty decision seemed worth the cost. Frobisher's vision ignited in the hearts of his countrymen, fifteen ships were filled with about three-hundred miners and sent to Canada as quickly as the ships could go. Frobisher did not even wait long enough to have the gold tested. En route, part of his fleet was lost and the ship that carried the lumber to build a settlement sank, leaving the crew having to endure the harsh elements of the arctic region in old wooden ships. Martin Frobisher's crew spent the entire summer gathering the ore and stowing it on board the remaining ships, working to the last minute. They barely escaped the clutches of an unforgiving winter. The summer conditions were so tough that some of the men deserted and returned home early. Despite the setbacks, Frobisher plunged forward, loading the ships dangerously full. Frobisher even exchanged the ballast of the ship for the ore the miners gathered. He returned to England with visions of grandeur and glory which quickly faded upon learning that the ore contained iron pyrite—fool's gold![3]

As Martin Frobisher's story shows us, things are not always as they seem. We can see what we want to see, instead of pursuing what God wants us to pursue. Ask God what He wants for your life. Diligently seek Him when you lack vision. If you have a vision, ask God if that is His vision for your life.

LIVING A VIRTUAL LIFE

It is possible to live so much in our own visions that we stop living in reality, going from one vision to another, preferring it to the reality of our lives. This lifestyle becomes as addictive as virtual reality. When you look back and see how little these visions produced compared to all the time, money, and effort you put into them, you will lose heart. Some console themselves by saying that they learned a lot along the way, but they paid a heavy price. While this consolation is not wrong, we should see that consolation and confirmation are not the same. Consolation is not confirmation that what we did out of our own will was really what God wanted for us.

One of the things that has tempered my own visionary tendency has been the number of people I have counselled who live from one self-generated vision to the next. These individuals complicate their lives, dishearten their loved one, and in time, discredit the Lord.

This lifestyle becomes as addictive as virtual reality.

10 CHARACTERISTICS OF A VISION FROM GOD

1. **God calls us to be something.** As I listen to people share their visions, they usually talk about doing, doing, doing. A vision that comes from God should also include what we are to be, not just what we are to do. Notice how Saul, on the road to Damascus, was being called to be a servant of Jesus Christ. All his doing came out of his being. For example, we need to ask ourselves questions like, what kind of Christian will I be? What kind of parent, partner, or pastor?

2. **A vision from God is usually something only He can bring to pass.** Listening to some people share their visions, I can't help but think their visions all lay within their own abilities to bring them to pass. How different from the vision God gives, which requires faith and becoming utterly dependent upon Him in order to see it realized! Real vision will often make us feel in over our heads.

3. **What God shows us will always be given in part.** When Saul had his vision on the road to Damascus, he was promised more details later (Acts 9:6). Getting a vision from God is more like a jigsaw puzzle. It is made up of little parts. You don't always see the entire picture, but you are given pieces as you go. This is what Paul meant when he wrote that we *"know in part"* (1 Corinthians 13:9). A real vision from the Lord will require that we seek Him more, not less.

4. **We will need to connect with others.** We should have an overarching vision set before us, but we need short-term steps to bring it to pass. In Paul's case, connecting with the right people, such as Ananias and Barnabas, were the steps that helped him come into his purpose in God. Connecting with key people is always an essential part in fulfilling our purpose.

5. **A real vision from the Lord will benefit the lives of others.** When I listen to some people tell me their vision and hear them talk about themselves, I quickly become skeptical that their vision is from God.

6. **God's vision is usually imparted in just a few seconds, but it generally takes a lifetime to completely come to pass.** Saul was told on the road to Damascus that he would testify before kings. The book of Acts spans nearly a thirty-year period, and it was near the end of the book that he finally stood before kings (Acts 9:15-16; 26:16-19).

7. **The route will always be different than we imagined.** When Paul eventually stood before kings, he probably had not imagined that he would be doing so from prison, in chains, or with a bent or broken body. The same could be said of others in the Bible, like Joseph, who had a vision of becoming great but could never have imagined the route that God would take him.

8. **Some people will prophesy to you about how easy the journey is going to be.** Yet when Paul was given a vision by the Lord, he was told that he would have to suffer much for Christ's name. Difficulties lay ahead, but the Lord promised to protect Paul. God promises the same for us.

9. **He is the God who calls "those things that are not, as though they were" (Romans 4:17).** What God calls us to may seem unlikely or even impossible. Who "Saul" was and who "Paul" was going to become were

polar opposites. This was also true of Aaron, whose God-given vision included him becoming the high priest of God's people. When we read the context of when this vision was given, he was actually leading God's people into sin.

10. **It will require dogged faithfulness.** We need to check on an annual basis to see if what we are doing is congruent with the original vision God gave us. As proof that we believe the vision is from the Lord, we should say no to those things that do not fit into its scope or assist in its fulfillment. The devil will often try to sidetrack us from doing the will of God.

OUR CHURCHES NEED VISION

I believe a local church should discover their purpose in the same way that an individual should. I believe God wrote a book for each local church, so they would fulfill something specific in their region. I believe we will be summoned to stand before the Lord both as individuals and then as churches to give an account for what He called us to do with the grace He gives us. This is the basic concept in the Parable of the Talents, which can apply to individuals as well as churches and ministries. Similarly, the seven churches in Asia Minor were judged in their letters collectively and promised great things if they overcame. The vision was given to the pastor but addressed the group.

> A church is like an individual in many ways.

A church is like an individual in many ways. Individuals have a history, a purpose, unique characteristics, strengths, weaknesses, gifts, and callings. Some individuals are poor and some are rich. Some individuals are small and some are big by design, all as God has willed. These characteristics all apply to churches. This should cause us to ask,

- Why are we located where we are?
- Why does God send people into our midst with specific gifts and abilities?
- Why does He give us certain financial means?
- What is it all for?
- Why is it that no one church has it all or can do everything by themselves?
- Why do we exist?
- Why did God create our local church?

Do you think our churches were created in the heart of God just to have meetings on Sunday? I hope not. That could not possibly satisfy us for very long. Our meetings can help us fulfill our purpose, but they are not the only reason God created churches. This is similar to the way the church building is not the vision; the building helps facilitate the vision. If the pastor's primary vision is constructing a new building, he will move on when it is completed (as many do), but if the building is *for* something, he will likely stay until that *something* is completed.

I cannot imagine the Lord sitting down to write a book for our churches, and all He writes is, "Meetings, meetings, and more meetings." I think He had more in mind than that, more imagination than that, and more at stake than Sunday meetings every week. He paid too high a price for us to limit our churches to meetings. Jesus had more in mind for our churches. His vision for churches was worth the price of dying on the cross for our sins and allowing so many saints to face persecution and death. His purpose for churches is greater than Sunday meetings once a week.

As churches, we need to find our purpose in God for our area and for our generation. What are we called to do? This is why we should never just copy the vision of another church. We have to press in to get a glimpse of what is written in heaven for us. The visions for our churches should never be something that we just made up because it sounded good, was affordable, or easy to achieve. The purposes for our churches should be specific and something we have grace to do.

For example, I often hear churches say that God has called them to be a hospital. Can you think of a church that is not called to help people recover? Can you imagine a church that is not called to help heal those who have been hurt? Would God need to prophesy something as basic as this? I hope not, as it would reflect badly on both the church and God. Neither do we need a vision for us to love one another or to get along. That comes standard with the package, although we sometimes forget that. I think our calling has to be more specific, something that benefits specific people and our specific location.

I believe it is the pastor's primary responsibility to seek God in order to find His purposes and lead the people into those purposes. A church board or congregation cannot find the vision of God. They may try, but they will all see something different, because it is not their God-given responsibility to find the vision for the church. It is the head that has the eyes, and therefore it is the pastor who needs to receive the vision. The head of the local church is a person, not a committee. Pastors must constantly assess if the church they oversee is on target. This takes more than "a wing and a prayer." In fact, it takes more prayer than most people are willing to commit to. It is easier to just implement programs or do what we see other churches doing, but it will never satisfy us at a heart level. We are made for something more.

ASSIGNMENT

You should write out your vision. The Bible gives examples of people who wrote out visions to make them plain:

His purpose for churches is greater than Sunday meetings once a week.

Then the Lord answered me and said: "Write the vision and make it plain on tablets, that he may run who reads it. For the vision is yet for an appointed time; But at the end it will speak, and it will not lie. Though the vision tarries, wait for it; because it will surely come, it will not tarry." (Habakkuk 2:2-3)

So often people define their purpose by what they *do*, as opposed to what they will *be*. If you were to itemize your vision, how much of it would be about what you hope to accomplish? Would it be just a long to-do list?

PART THREE: GOD'S ULTIMATE AND IMMEDIATE WILL

I often hear people asking, "What is God's will for my life?" That question is a bit difficult to answer in that our lives are not one-dimensional. Neither is the will of God. I do not believe that God has one big will that covers all of my life. Our lives are made for many different purposes.

For example, you may have included God in choosing the job you now have but not in choosing the church you attend. I may have asked Him to help choose the right church to attend but not the car I should drive. You may have included Him in choosing the car you purchased but not the one you are to marry. However, if you marry someone without acknowledging the Lord but prayed more about what car to buy, your life is going to be a very long drive.

When trying to discern God's will, we have to begin by sorting out the difference between God's *ultimate will* and His *immediate will*. It is possible to pray according to His ultimate will yet be out of step with His immediate will. Let me explain.

Ultimately, the will of God is what He has laid out for us in the Bible. As we align our lives with the principles, priorities, and promises written in His Word, we will come into more of what He has willed for us. When we act according to what we read in the Bible, a lot of our decisions are made for us.

For example, someone may be wondering if it is God's will to be in a relationship with a certain person, who happens to be an unbeliever. The Bible already speaks about this, telling us that we are not to be unequally yoked with unbelievers (2 Corinthians 6:14). This makes our decision for us as we try to discern the will of God.

FINDING GOD'S IMMEDIATE WILL

The key to finding God's immediate will is to allow the Holy Spirit to show us how to pray. He can show us if there is a root problem or any steps that we need to take in order to see His will come to pass. To find God's immediate will, we need to allow the Holy Spirit to pray *through* us.

> *Likewise the Spirit also helps in our weaknesses. For we do not know what we should pray for as we ought, but the Spirit Himself makes intercession for us with groanings which cannot be uttered. Now He who searches the hearts knows what the mind of the Spirit is, because He makes intercession for the saints according to the will of God.* (Romans 8:26-27)

The Spirit can show us how to pray the mind of the Lord for ourselves and for those we care about. He can do this as we yield to Him, letting Him intercede through us in our own language, through groanings, or through tongues. When I do these things, I have found myself praying things I never thought before. Sometimes, my head balks at what my spirit is praying by the Spirit. He knows what the will of God is and can bring it from heaven to Earth, but it must be prayed through someone. He does not do it on His own.

When the Lord does speak to us, faith comes, which is what we need to see His will brought into being:

So then faith comes by hearing, and hearing by the word of God. (Romans 10:17)

The term *word of God* used here is the *rhema* of God, which is God speaking to us in our specific situation today. The *rhema* contains the faith we need to be healed. As the Word says, *"He sent His word and healed them"* (Psalm 107:20).

The only way to know how to get God's ultimate will into our immediate circumstance is to ask the Lord to show us and to seek Him in our time of need. In the end, finding God's immediate will always comes out of our relationship with Him.

God's ultimate will does not come about automatically. His will must be procured, insisted upon, by faith and by our importunity. This is what Jesus taught when the disciples asked Him to teach them to pray in Luke 11:5-8.

As we submit our will to His, asking Him to choose what would bring Him pleasure instead of what we want, we will begin to see His ultimate will come into being in our immediate circumstances.

Jesus had to go to a deeper level of submission while He was praying about the cross:

He went a little farther, and fell on the ground, and prayed that if it were possible, the hour might pass from Him. And He said, "Abba, Father, all things are possible for You. Take this cup away from Me; nevertheless, not what I will, but what You will." (Mark 14:36)

We will have to surrender the same way at times, knowing that what would please Him is going to be painful for us, we need to understanding that no one has done this to the degree He did.

You can hear this same kind of tension in trusting God when the three young Hebrew men were told that, if they didn't bow down and worship the golden statue, they would be thrown into the fiery furnace:

Shadrach, Meshach, and Abed-Nego answered and said to the king, "O Nebuchadnezzar, we have no need to answer you in this matter. If that is the case, our God whom we serve is able to deliver us from the burning fiery furnace, and He will deliver us from your hand, O king. But if not, let it be known to you, O king, that we do not serve your gods, nor will we worship the gold image which you have set up." (Daniel 3:16-18)

> God's ultimate will does not come about automatically.

LEAVING THE CHOICE TO HIM

When it comes to getting guidance, we must have the same attitude Jesus and the three young Hebrew men had. It is helpful if you are familiar with Scripture, but this will not help you decide which car to buy. For that, you will need to know God's voice, which again, comes out of relationship.

One time, I felt it was time to get a newer vehicle but was not sure which type to get. I had been driving a big van but wasn't sure if I needed that same size vehicle at this new stage of my life. I didn't know if I would still be taking people with me on long trips or if I should get a small car with better fuel economy. I simply did not know what kind of car would suit me best, but I knew Jesus held the future and He knew what was best for me, so I asked Him to show me which car to buy. Anytime I wondered about which car to buy, I would simply ask Him to show me what was best for me. I asked Him to choose. I felt I was in the right vein when I prayed this way.

Then one day, as I was driving down the highway, a car passed me but seemed to hang right ahead of me for some time. The car caught my attention, and I found myself looking it over more than I usually would. It had several features I liked, and as I prayed, I found myself saying, "Lord, I will take that kind of car." Within a couple of days, I was driving a car just like that one. It turned out to be the perfect car for Heather and me for many years and never had an issue, other than regular maintenance.

SWEET SURRENDER

> I felt this plan would put my ministry on a dead-end street.

Another time, I had been earnestly seeking the Lord for direction but was not liking the guidance I was getting. To my mind, it seemed like the Lord was leading me the wrong way. What God was telling me to do seemed backward to me. His vision was contrary to my sense of ambition and concern of what others would think. I felt this plan would put my ministry on a dead-end street. I even told a friend who I was staying with that I felt I must have done something wrong because it seemed like God was banishing me to the boonies. When I got up in the middle of night to go to the bathroom, the Lord spoke to me. He did it in an interesting way. I had noticed that the bathroom door had been held open by a large round piece of glass, similar in size and shape as a cereal bowl. It looked like someone had cut out a greeting card and stuck it under the glass, which magnified the card. I could read the script when I got down on my knees. When I got down to read the card, I was struck by what it said:

"God always gives His best to those who leave the choice with Him." [4]

It was a quote taken from the life of Jim Elliot, who must have wrestled with God's choice for his ministry at some point too. I could sense God's presence as I surrendered right then and there on my knees in the middle of the night. I gave up trying to be in control of my life and what other people thought of me. He wanted me to go to this place, I would go, leaving the choice to Him.

As it turned out, it was God's direction, and I soon found out that it was one of the best moves I could have made, full of long-standing relationships that I have enjoyed to this day.

In Psalm 47:2-4, the writer said that the great King will choose our inheritance for us:

> *For the Lord Most High is awesome; He is a great King over all the earth. He will subdue the peoples under us, And the nations under our feet. He will choose our inheritance for us, the excellence of Jacob whom He loves. Selah*

God still does this, if we will let Him. If the Lord is going to choose our inheritance for us, then we need to let Him. Perhaps this is why the Bible says,

> *"For thus says the Lord: "To the eunuchs who keep My Sabbaths, And choose what pleases Me, And hold fast My covenant, Even to them I will give in My house And within My walls a place and a name Better than that of sons and daughters; I will give them an everlasting name That shall not be cut off." (Isaiah 56:4-5)*

Our prayer of surrender to God's will must simply be, *"Choose, thou, for me, O God!"*

The next morning, I was full of peace. I was excited about what lay ahead. The future looked promising and my soul was satisfied with the taste of sweet surrender. I took the position that had been offered to me and it became such a great blessing to my family, my life, and ministry. I can relate to the old John Denver song called "Sweet Surrender," where he wrote,

> Lost and alone on some forgotten highway, traveled by many, remembered by few. Looking for something that I can believe in, looking for something that I'd like to do with my life. There's nothing behind me and nothing that ties me to something that might have been true yesterday. Tomorrow is open and right now it seems to be more than enough. To just be here today, and I don't know what the future is holding in store, I don't know where I'm going, I'm not sure where I've been. There's a spirit that guides me, a light that shines for me, my life is worth the living, I don't need to see the end. Sweet, sweet surrender, live, live without care, like a fish in the water, like a bird in the air. Sweet, sweet surrender, live, live without care, like a fish in the water, like a bird in the air.[5]

> **The future looked promising and my soul was satisfied with the taste of sweet surrender.**

WHEN STUFF HAPPENS TO ME THAT GOD COULD NOT HAVE WILLED

One thing that helps me surrender readily, especially when I don't fully understand what God is requiring of me, has been the words Paul wrote in Romans 8:28-30:

And we know that all things work together for good to those who love God, to those who are the called according to His purpose. For whom He foreknew, He also predestined to be conformed to the image of His Son, that He might be the firstborn among many brethren. Moreover whom He predestined, these He also called; whom He called, these He also justified; and whom He justified, these He also glorified.

This is one of the most amazing promises in the Bible. Paul learned by experience this inner assurance: If we are sincerely seeking to do God's will, then He has a way of turning everything around for our benefit. We are beloved and called according to His purpose. Even when something happens that God has not willed for me, it can be used by Him to further my purpose. This means even when I have been self-willed, yet repentant, He will "sweep up" after me. This means that, even when the enemy gets the upper hand and his will hurts my life, God will make sure that it turns out for my good. Even if the will of man prevails in some circumstance, negatively affecting me, God's will is so all-encompassing that anything can be redeemed for a higher purpose. We must be humble and repentant when we make a mistake or rebel against God's will for our lives.

> **Even when something happens that God has not willed for me, it can be used by Him to further my purpose.**

LITTLE CHOICES—BIG CONSEQUENCES

There are little things, which seem to be inconsequential in themselves, but they can have great consequences for our lives. There are a number of examples of these little things throughout Scripture. Sometimes these "inconsequential" things are good, and sometimes, they are bad. One of my favorite good examples is found in the life of Rebekah, who became the wife of Isaac.

When Rebekah was a teenager, she came to the well each evening to draw water for the night. She was just one among a group of girls whose daily chore was to walk down into the cold well and haul water. This was hard, strenuous work. I have seen this done in India many times and marvel at how gracefully these women get the water, even though it is cold, wet, and exhausting work.

On this particular day, a stranger stood in the distance, in front of a large group of camels. When all the other girls headed home with their haul, Rebekah was the only teenager who decided to act on an unwritten law that said it pleased God for His people to treat a stranger with kindness. She went and asked if the stranger would like a cup of water and asked if she could also water his camels. This would not be easy because these animals can really put away water. She didn't offer water because it was easy, but because it was the right thing to do. Little did she know that the stranger had just been praying, saying,

> *"O Lord God of my master Abraham, please give me success this day, and show kindness to my master Abraham. Behold, here I stand by the well of water, and the daughters of the men of the city are coming out to draw water. Now let it be that the young woman to whom I say, 'Please let down your pitcher that I may drink,' and she says, 'Drink, and I will also give your camels a drink'—let her be the one You have appointed for Your servant Isaac. And by this I will know that You have shown kindness to my master."* (Genesis 24:12-14)

When Rebekah came forward to offer water, she could never have imagined that it would lead to her soon becoming a bride to one of the richest men on the earth. Isaac was not only the heir of all that Abraham had, but an heir to the promise of God's blessing.

GIVING AWAY RAZOR BLADES

I experienced something similar to Rebecca one time, while teaching for a week at a Bible school. I happened to notice how one of the students, a young man from India named Hemant, had started to grow a beard. I joked with him about it, thinking he was doing it because of the change in climate or the fact that he was away from his wife for such a long time. He laughed at my teasing him, but I could see a hurt flash across his eyes. It was a micro-reaction, lasting only part of a second, but I saw it.

Later that day, I went to his room to see what was the matter. He was surprised to see me at his door, saying I was the first person to ever come to his room to check on him. It was then I discovered that he didn't have any more razor blades or much of anything else, either. It was as if he were in a prison cell. He was also desperately homesick.

When I went back to Lowville, our church put together a "care package" for him with lots of supplies and goodies in it. When we found he had no place to go during the month-long Christmas break, my family invited him to come to our home.

It was fun having Hemant around. We took him skating and sledding, and the kids often hiked with him around in the knee-deep snow, something he had never done before. We introduced him to our special Christmas food and enjoyed sitting around the table at night, telling stories. He told us stories about life in the jungle of India. He told us about a primitive tribe he had visited in the mountains of Orissa. He said they lived deep in the forest, surviving off the land the way people lived thousands of years ago. They were called "untouchables"

The prospect of it was both exciting and frightening.

and were virtually unrecognized by their government. Hemant told us how some young men he knew had gone into the jungle to tell them about Jesus and had even planted churches among them, even though they were stoned and were refused food or shelter. He said they desperately needed Bible teaching and asked me if I would come to India to help them. This was an idea I had never considered before. The prospect of it was both exciting and frightening. Little did I realize this invitation would lead to one of the richest experiences of my life.

In 1992, I traveled to India and spent a large part of my time there, going through the jungle mountains on the back of a motorcycle with Hemant. We went from one remote jungle village to another, preaching to and praying for people. Many wonderful things happened as I walked among the tribal people in Jesus' name. A great conviction preceded every meeting, and a great joy was left in our wake. Many people gained new freedom because of God's free-flowing salvation, deliverance, and healing. I was having the time of my life.

This first trip resulted in my going to India regularly for over the next twenty years. I met brothers like Gabriel Pradhan and Dillip Nayak, who would become my partners in ministry for India. Together, we have built a ministry there that the nationals manage themselves. It's called *Word of Grace Fellowship of India*. Our focus has been on reaching and building up the tribal people who have come to know the Lord. The work has grown significantly since then and has been blessed by the Lord in every way. To think that it all started by giving a care package.

ASSIGNMENT

In order to see Romans 8:28-30 at work in someone's life, get to know Abraham, Isaac, and Jacob. As you walk with them on their journey in the book of Genesis, you will see things happen to them that were the result of their own self-will, or the will of someone else, yet God ultimately turned it around for their benefit, posterity, and His own purposes.

Abraham had to surrender to the will of God in sacrificing his only son. It would also help if you studied Paul's perspective about Abraham's life in Romans 4.

PART FOUR: DISCERNING THE WILL OF GOD

As we begin sorting out what the will of God is for our lives, we soon discover that it is a serious discerning process. In order to discern God's will, we need to keep in mind that we also have a will, the devil has a will, and other people have a will and they are trying to get us to yield our will to theirs.

Beyond this, we need to factor in that our own flesh and spirit are in a constant battle over who is going to be in control of our will, which is based in our soul. This makes it difficult to trust our feelings.

The devil, who is called the "god of this world" is at work in the earth and can manipulate circumstances. Because of this, circumstances become less reliable factors in discerning the will of God. Circumstances can be deceiving, yet we tend to rely heavily upon them for guidance. This is why we must *pray* that God's will be done.

Some naively conclude that if their circumstances are easy, it is an indication of being in God's will. This conclusion is just as naive as the conclusion that hardship or conflict is an indication that it must be the devil's will. We have to get past the simplicity that says, "Only good experiences come from God and only bad things come from the devil."

If this were true, how do we explain the following?

- Jesus was in the will of God but faced countless hardships. He was in the will of God when the storm came up on the Sea of Galilee, almost swamping the boat. Yet, He could sleep in the back of the boat on a pillow, resting in God's purpose for His life.

- Joseph was trying to move toward a vision God had given him. The doors God opened led him down a well, to an auction block, and into a dungeon.

- As we read 2 Corinthians 12, we see the list of hardships Paul suffered as he did the will of God. This included multiple shipwrecks, time in prison, going without food or clothing, and going without money.

The will of God is not having smooth or synchronized circumstances, as much as it is fulfilling God's purposes in spite of the circumstances.

Another area where we need to mature is in the area of bargains or freebies. We somehow think if it is on sale or free that it must be of God. Many (myself included) who have looked for confirmation in these things have been misguided.

As a young disciple, I was trying to get a new business off the ground when I met an old business acquaintance who had offered me some office space in his building. It was a beautiful office, complete with furniture and even the

> Some naively conclude that if their circumstances are easy, it is an indication of being in God's will.

special equipment I would need to do the kind of work I had in mind, and it was all free of charge. I showed the business space to a couple of other Christian artists, whose skillset I needed to do what I had envisioned. We talked about how they might need to quit their jobs to come work for me in my new enterprise, even though I had not a single customer nor made a single dollar. The couple felt hesitant and finally told me they would not be joining me. This got my attention. Before they did this, from my visionary view of life, everything looked like the Lord's leading, meeting people just at the right time, loads of free stuff, finding people with the skillsets needed. But none of it was the Lord. As it turned out, I was about a year too early and needed to start on a smaller scale. I had to humble myself, admit my errors, and go back to waiting upon the Lord. This was the first time I had to learn that not everything that is free is from the Lord, and it was not to be my last.

A few years later, I had grown discontent with my business and felt in my heart that a change was coming soon. I had been waiting for the Lord to release me into the ministry, and was diligently prepared for this, but after waiting so long, it seemed like it would never happen. After all, it had been five years of constant preparation, but no real full-time opportunity was apparent to me. I felt that I either needed to expand my business or go into ministry—something had to happen. I had a nice, little affordable downtown office but decided to lease something much bigger, more expensive, and more visible, which I thought would cause my business to expand. I also got some special equipment, all of which required signing a long-term lease. I had gone through the motions of seeking counsel, including talking to the leadership of the church I attended, but at a heart level was not really open to anything they might say that would contradict my plans. I only heard what I wanted to hear. They must have sensed this too, so they were not as direct with me as they could have been until it was almost too late. When they finally shared their concerns and objections, I knew I had somehow missed God's will and had to stop everything, but it was costly to do so. In the end, a door to full-time ministry soon opened for me, but the Lord made me pay on all those leases up to the last penny.

TESTING TO SEE IF SOMETHING IS THE WILL OF GOD

In Romans 12:2, Paul told the believers in Rome to *"prove"* what is *"that good, and acceptable and perfect will of God."* Today, we would say *test* or *discern*.

The apostle Paul told the Romans that the will of God needed to be discerned. God's will was not obvious; they had to test it. This takes time, effort, and integrity. To *prove* or *discern* means:

- to test, examine, prove, scrutinize (to see whether a thing is genuine or not), as metals

- to recognize as genuine after examination, to approve, deem worthy

We do not use these words much today, but the idea behind the word *proving* is *assaying*. An *assayer* is a person who tests ores and minerals and analyzes them to determine their composition and value. It is a laborious and time-consuming process. You will never offend God by assaying your guidance. Turn it over, tap on it, shake it really well. You will never make Him angry by sincerely questioning it. You should question it. Asking for further clarity is not an act of doubt or a lack of faith in Him. It is a wise thing to do.

In order to "discern" the will of God, we will need to do a number of things:

1. We must ask ourselves if what we are about to do will bring pleasure to God.

2. We must ask ourselves what form of pleasure we would get out of such a decision. Would it bring pleasure to our flesh or to our spirit?

3. We must ask ourselves if it contradicts what is already clearly His will as revealed in His written Word.

4. We must ask ourselves if it is in keeping with what He has already made known to us or previously confirmed. Is the new guidance we have received in keeping with the original vision, prophecy, or calling that has been given to us? There should be a logical progression to God's guidance because He does all things decently and in order. He is not all over the map, changing His mind every other day, contrary to what some believe.

5. We must ask ourselves, who stands to benefit most from the decision? God does not grace our selfishness.

6. We must ask ourselves what we will have to compromise to get what we are seeking. Some people trade their integrity or moral authority for lesser things. Others trade something they have, such as their children, their marriage, or their health, in order to try to get a hold of something that they can never reach. This brings no pleasure to God.

> **You will never offend God by assaying your guidance.**

GOD'S WILL IS HIS PLEASURE

One of the things that help us begin to discern the will of God is to always try to please the Lord. The Apostle John came back from heaven with a revelation that we were all made for God's pleasure:

Thou art worthy, O Lord, to receive glory and honour and power: for thou hast created all things, and for thy pleasure they are and were created. (Revelation 4:11 KJV)

This same verse is translated in the New King James Version as:

You are worthy, O Lord, to receive glory and honor and power; for You created all things, and by Your will they exist and were created.

Notice how the word *pleasure* and *will* are used interchangeably in these two translations. That is because the Greek word for both is *thelema*. According to the *Strong's Concordance* the word *thelema* (GK. 2307) means a determination, a choice, specifically, a purpose, decree, or inclination. It is often translated as *desire* or *pleasure*. So, one way to understand what God's will may be for our lives, is by changing the word *will* to:

- His pleasure
- His desire
- His purpose
- His choice

In this one verse, we can see what we were created for. We will find our purposes as we begin to seek to please Him. It is important if we are going to begin to understand what God's will is, to know what brings Him pleasure.

Here are some other verses that link His will and His pleasure together:

Having predestined us to adoption as sons by Jesus Christ to Himself, according to the good pleasure of His will. (Ephesians 1:5)

Having made known to us the mystery of His will, according to His good pleasure which He purposed in Himself. (v. 9)

For it is God who works in you both to will and to do for His good pleasure. (Philippians 2:13)

From these Scriptures, we can see how God's will is His pleasure. Since we were created by and for His pleasure, it is safe to conclude that our own pleasure, or personal happiness and fulfillment, is directly tied to doing what pleases the Father.

In John 8:28-29, Jesus said that He always does whatever pleases the Father:

When you lift up the Son of Man, then you will know that I am He, and that I do nothing of Myself; but as My Father taught Me, I speak these things. And He who sent Me is with Me. The Father has not left Me alone, for I always do those things that please Him.

He also said He came to do His Father's will:

For I have come down from heaven, not to do My own will, but the will of Him who sent Me. (John 6:38)

Again, both of these things are the same thing. God's will (*thelema*) is His pleasure (*thelema*).

For that matter, our *will* is also our *pleasure*. Doing whatever we want to do, living to please ourselves, is called being self-willed which is the very thing that keeps us from coming into our God-ordained purpose. We miss out on the truly great quests in life when we follow our own will rather than God's will.

There is a great contest between doing our will or doing God's will; pleasing ourselves or pleasing Him. If I could convince you of one thing, it would be that your heart's desire, your deepest pleasure, or a sense of satisfaction in this life, can be found only in doing what brings Him pleasure. It is when we press past our prejudices, our penchant for comfort, or our need to have the approval of others, that we can tap into the will of God. It is only then that we will find our own fulfillment which comes from discovering and doing what we were created to do. We were made to do something, and until we begin walking in it, we will never feel complete.

> It is when we press past our prejudices, our penchant for comfort, or our need to have the approval of others, that we can tap into the will of God.

WHAT BRINGS GOD PLEASURE?

In terms of the ultimate will of God, the Scripture tells us these three things please the Lord:

1. **It is His will or pleasure that we walk with Him in sonship:**

   Blessed be the God and Father of our Lord Jesus Christ, who has blessed us with every spiritual blessing in the heavenly places in Christ, just as He chose us in Him before the foundation of the world, that we should be holy and without blame before Him in love, having predestined us to adoption as sons by Jesus Christ to Himself, according to the good pleasure of His will, to the praise of the glory of His grace, by which He has made us accepted in the Beloved. (Ephesians 1:3-6)

2. **It is His will that we walk out the Kingdom:**

   "But seek the kingdom of God, and all these things shall be added to you. Do not fear, little flock, for it is your Father's good pleasure to give you the kingdom." (Luke 12:31-32)

3. **It is His will that we continue to walk by faith:**

   Now the just shall live by faith; but if anyone draws back, My soul has no pleasure in him. But we are not of those who draw back to perdition, but of those who believe to the saving of the soul. (Hebrews 10:38-39)

We will need to focus on these three things in order to come into more of God's will for our lives.

WHAT DELIGHTS HIS HEART?

Of course, there are degrees of pleasure, from things we like to things we love. The highest level of pleasure is called *delight*. One definition I found was, "a feeling of extreme pleasure or satisfaction." This is what happens whenever we experience something that is truly delicious to our souls. We find ourselves closing our eyes to block everything else out so we can fully take it in. It is what happens when you find yourself smiling at the anticipation of experiencing that thing again. While there are many things we enjoy, there are few things in life that we could really classify as a delight.

Here are some things that God delights in:

- **His list of delights is different than man's list.**

    "Thus says the Lord, Let not the wise man glory in his wisdom, neither let the mighty man glory in his might, let not the rich man glory in his riches: But let him that glories glory in this, that he understands and knows me, that I am the Lord which does lovingkindness, judgment, and righteousness, in the earth: for in these things I delight, says the Lord." (Jeremiah 9:23-24)

- **God delights in mercy.**

    Who is a God like You, pardoning iniquity and passing over the transgression of the remnant of His heritage? He does not retain His anger forever, because He delights in mercy. (Micah 7:18)

- **God delights in those who hope in His mercy.**

    The Lord takes pleasure in those who fear Him, in those who hope in His mercy. (Psalm 147:11)

- **God delights in our prayers and worship.**

    The sacrifice of the wicked is an abomination to the Lord: but the prayer (or the hymn) of the upright is his delight. (Proverbs 15:8)

- **God delights in obedience.**

    So Samuel said: "Has the Lord as great delight in burnt offerings and sacrifices, as in obeying the voice of the Lord? Behold, to obey is better than sacrifice, and to heed than the fat of rams." (1 Samuel 15:22)

- **God delights in wisdom.**

    And I was daily His delight, rejoicing always before Him, rejoicing in His inhabited world, and my delight was with the sons of men. (Proverbs 8:30-31)

- **God delights in those who relate to others with honesty.**

    Lying lips are an abomination to the Lord, but those who deal truthfully are His delight. (Proverbs 12:22)

A LIST OF GOD'S PRIORITIES

We can often come into the will of God by aligning our lives with God's priorities as revealed in His Word. What do you think God's priorities are? How would they compare with yours? While the word *priority* may not often appear in Scripture, it is communicated in the word *first*. Here is the Greek definition of the word *first* taken from the *Strong's Concordance*:

> **FIRST** 4412 GK. *proton* from GK 4413; firstly (in time, place, order, or importance): before, at the beginning, chiefly, (at, at the) first (of all).

The following Scriptures give us an indication of what some of God's priorities are. From this, we are able to determine what our priorities should be.

We are to love the Lord.

Then one of them, a lawyer, asked Him a question, testing Him, and saying, "Teacher, which is the great commandment in the law?" Jesus said to him, "You shall love the Lord your God with all your heart, with all your soul, and with all your mind. This is the first and great commandment. And the second is like it: You shall love your neighbor as yourself. On these two commandments hang all the Law and the Prophets." (Matthew 22:35-40)

We are able to measure the depth of our love for God in several ways.

1. **By how we do what His Word says or what He has spoken to us:**

    But whoever keeps His word, truly the love of God is perfected in him. By this we know that we are in Him. (1 John 2:5)

2. **By how we give to those in need:**

    But whoever has this world's goods, and sees his brother in need, and shuts up his heart from him, how does the love for God abide in him? (1 John 3:17)

3. **By how we love people:**

    If someone says, "I love God," and hates his brother, he is a liar; for he who does not love his brother whom he has seen, how can he love God whom he has not seen? And this commandment we have from Him: that he who loves God must love his brother also. (1 John 4:20-21)

4. **By how we prioritize reconciliation and relationships:**

    "Leave your gift at the altar and go your way. First be reconciled to your brother, and then come and offer your gift." (Matthew 5:24)

    Reconciliation is so important to God that He would rather have it than your worship or offerings.

5. **By how we put the Kingdom first:**

   "But seek first the kingdom of God and His righteousness, and all these things shall be added to you." (Matthew 6:33)

   Jesus said the Kingdom of God was within us. This means we have to set our spiritual lives and the spiritual lives of others as our highest priority.

6. **By how we judge ourselves first:**

   "Hypocrite! First remove the plank from your own eye, and then you will see clearly to remove the speck from your brother's eye." (Matthew 7:5)

   When you see a problem in someone that seems intolerable to you, it is your cue to step back to see where this same thing might be in your life. Change yourself, and then you will have something to say to help others.

7. **By how we prioritize getting the gospel out**:

   "And the gospel must first be preached to all the nations." (Mark 13:10)

   This is not His responsibility, but ours. What are you doing to make the gospel known?

8. **By how we prioritize being a disciple:**

   Then He said to another, "Follow Me." But he said, "Lord, let me first go and bury my father." Jesus said to him, "Let the dead bury their own dead, but you go and preach the kingdom of God." And another also said, "Lord, I will follow You, but let me first go and bid them farewell who are at my house." But Jesus said to him, "No one, having put his hand to the plow, and looking back, is fit for the kingdom of God." (Luke 9:59-62)

   To be a disciple means we have to prioritize our lives around following Him, even above our familial interests. The pendulum can swing both ways on this issue; we can also neglect our families' concerns before serving the Lord. Only by following Him can we find the balance in this.

9. **By how we prioritize giving:**

   For I bear witness that according to their ability, yes, and beyond their ability, they were freely willing, imploring us with much urgency that we would receive the gift and the fellowship of the ministering to the saints. And not only as we had hoped, but they first gave themselves to the Lord, and then to us by the will of God. (2 Corinthians 8:3-5)

The people at Macedonia were so poor, yet they asked, with urgency, to be allowed to give to others in need. The way they entered into this level of giving was by first giving themselves to the Lord. Once He has you, anything else you have is secondary.

10. By how we prioritize praying for others:

Therefore I exhort first of all that supplications, prayers, intercessions, and giving of thanks be made for all men, for kings and all who are in authority, that we may lead a quiet and peaceable life in all godliness and reverence. (1 Timothy 2:1-2)

At times, our love for praying for our leaders has been offset by our love for criticism. Instead of arm-chair quarterbacking, we must get on our knees and bury our heads in the chair, praying fervently for our president, governors, and other governmental leaders.

11. By how we prioritize our first love:

"Nevertheless I have this against you, that you have left your first love. Remember therefore from where you have fallen; repent and do the first works, or else I will come to you quickly and remove your lampstand from its place; unless you repent." (Revelation 2:4-5)

The most amazing thing about this is this church was so busy *doing* church and various ministries that they did not fully realize they had left their love for the Lord. The first works are the things we did as new believers, loving to spend time with Him, singing to Him, walking and talking to Him, inquiring of Him, and eagerly learning everything we could about Him by personal experience.

KNOWING THE DEPTH OF HIS LOVE

What if our aim was to become the most loving people possible? What if we were to make knowing and experiencing God's love become our greatest quest in life? The apostle John stated that God is love (1 John 4:8). This makes love eternal, which means there is no end to the pursuit of love. As we set out to love others, we find ourselves walking the halls of His heart, exploring Him, knowing Him by experience, and letting Him flow through us to others. Could there be anything higher than this? Or more fulfilling? Now that's a quest worthy of giving our lives for, even though there is no category for it in the *Guinness Book of World Records*.

The apostle Paul said something similar to the Corinthians, when he wrote,

Pursue love, and desire spiritual gifts, but especially that you may prophesy. (1 Corinthians 14:1)

In doing this, he revealed what he felt were the highest goals in life, pointing us toward the pursuit of love and grace, both of which would require that we live our lives for the benefit others.

Love and grace are biblically linked in the verse above. Reading this verse in the Amplified Bible gives us a picture of the greatest quest we could ever go on:

Eagerly pursue and seek to acquire [this] love [make it your aim, your great quest]; and earnestly desire and cultivate the spiritual endowments (gifts), especially that you may prophesy (interpret the divine will and purpose in inspired preaching and teaching).

This quest is so simple that we often overlook it, but I cannot think of another that is more difficult to do, which perhaps is why it is not on the top of most people's things to *be* list.

> **I believe God has a distinct purpose for each of us.**

I believe God has a distinct purpose for each of us. It is our responsibility, and should be our great quest in life, to find out what He wrote about us in His books. The entire content of the books He wrote will be revealed on the day when we stand before Him, but until then, we can get glimpses of what He wrote with the eyes of our heart. This will enable us to live for Him in His will for our lives. Not only can we know God's will, but we *need to* know it. Our heart's satisfaction depends upon it. It is the key to our fulfillment as a person. Knowing His preordained purpose for our lives takes a lifetime to achieve, so we need to begin here and now. This has been one of my great pursuits in life. I want to dedicate a sizeable portion of this study guide to helping you understand what the will of God is and know some of the guidelines that have made coming into it much easier for me.

PART FIVE: ASKING, SEEKING, AND KNOCKING

In some Asian or Middle Eastern cultures, it is offensive to go to someone's house and immediately begin asking them for something. For example, if you needed a wrench and asked your neighbor to borrow one, you would have to sit for a while. Your neighbor would ask about your family, perhaps your health, or talk about the weather. After a while, your neighbor would ask you what you needed and then you would ask to borrow a wrench, which they would gladly give you.

I think God is more Middle Eastern than we realize. He wants us to spend time with Him; He wants us to talk with Him before we ask for things. He wants to build a relationship more than He wants to give us the answers we want.

Jesus told the woman at the well an amazing revelation about the Father. Jesus revealed how the Father was always seeking those who worship Him in spirit and in truth (John 4:23). This means the Father is longing and looking for those who will spend time with Him with open hearts. He is looking for anyone with honest questions and honest doubts, and anyone who is honest about their true condition. The woman at the well's life was a wreck; she had had multiple romantic relationships without finding fulfillment. She had given up on marriage and was living with someone—but God still sought to have a relationship with her. God wanted her and told her so.

In the same way, God demonstrated His desire to have a relationship with Adam. God would come down to Eden to be with Adam. I don't think the Lord came down and began with, "Which animals did you name today? How many did you get through?" It wasn't all about Adam's work. God simply wanted to spend time with Adam.

Rather than spending all our time in prayer, talking about our wants or what we want God to do for us, we should want to spend time worshiping Him. God wants your heart and desires your sincere worship. You were created for His pleasure. The direction and purpose you have been longing for will flow out of an intimate relationship with Christ.

LEARNING TO ASK

When Jesus was teaching the disciples to pray, He told them to ask for God's will in heaven to come to earth (Matthew 6:9-13). He then went on to tell them how they should ask, seek, and knock—which I believe were intended to be the steps for us to find His immediate will for our everyday lives. Jesus said,

> *Ask, and it will be given to you; seek, and you will find; knock, and it will be opened to you. For everyone who asks receives, and he who seeks finds, and to him who knocks it will be opened. Or what man is there among you who, if his son asks for bread, will give him a stone? Or if he*

I think God is more Middle Eastern than we realize.

asks for a fish, will he give him a serpent? If you then, being evil, know how to give good gifts to your children, how much more will your Father who is in heaven give good things to those who ask Him! Therefore, whatever you want men to do to you, do also to them, for this is the Law and the Prophets. (Matthew 7:7-12)

GENUINE MOOSE-HIDE MOCCASINS

Many people are often reluctant to ask God for anything. It is as if we believe He is not really willing to answer our questions or meet our needs. We lose sight of how open and present He is. I had to learn the lesson of God's desire to meet our needs all over again recently. I think this reality is something we need to rediscover again and again, no matter how old we are in the Lord.

My wife, Heather, and I were making our way home from a vacation where we had cruised on a ship up the coasts of New England and Canada. Every time the ship came into a different port, we walked all over the respective port town each day we were there. As we were driving home, I noticed how much my feet ached. I enjoyed walking but didn't have the right kind of shoes on when we had walked. So now, as I was driving, I was really feeling it. As we drove home, we passed a sign advertising an outlet store that only sold genuine moose-hide moccasins. I knew these slippers were one of the most comfortable things you could ever put on your feet. Years before, I had tried on a pair but couldn't afford to buy them, but I never forgotten how great they were. Now that my feet were aching, I said to myself, *"Ah, if only I could sink my old feet into a pair of those genuine moose-hide moccasins."*

To my surprise, a voice within me said, as calm and cool as could be, "You have not because you ask not."

I was shocked.

I could hardly believe what I heard, and I knew it was not my voice, because it seemed to come out of nowhere rather than from my natural line of thinking. Also, it was a totally different tone from the tone I usually think to myself in. I know the words spoken were in the Bible but could not remember the specific reference. After some time, I realized it was from James 1:3. With this thought came the sense that I was free to ask for genuine moose-hide moccasins.

As Heather sat beside me, unaware of what was going on inside me, I became fully alert. I began to pray, "Father, could I ask for something like this? It is not a need, just something I would like." The sense I got was that I didn't have the slippers because I hadn't asked for them. It really created a dilemma for me, but then it was almost a challenge of faith. I prayed, slowly and deliberately, "Lord, I would like a pair of genuine moose-hide moccasins. Thank You for providing them."

> I could hardly believe what I heard.

We were well past the outlet store by this point in our journey but came to a red light beside a large second-hand store. As I turned my head to look at the store, I instinctively knew that my moccasins were in that store. After taking a minute to process this, I asked my wife if she wanted to stop and look around the store. She normally would not hesitate to do this, but this time she was too tired and just wanted to get home. I sat there for another minute, growing excited about the prospect that my answer to prayer was just a few feet away. I said, "Let's go in for a few minutes, just to stretch our legs."

She agreed, and I excitedly wheeled right in and made a beeline to the shoe department. As I scanned the rows of almost every kind of shoe imaginable, I stopped and looked down at a pair of new moccasins. They still had the trademark leather tag on them that proudly proclaimed them to be genuine moose-hide moccasins. They were available for five dollars! I picked them up, almost in disbelief, and marveled at the entire process, which now had been going on for the last half-hour. I felt beloved and moved that God would not only answer my prayer so profoundly, but almost dare me to pray it in the first place. Then I noticed another pair and scooped them up as well. I walked out of the store with two pairs! I ditched my worn-out sneakers and sat behind the wheel. My heart was stirred almost to tears the rest of the way home, and even for months afterward—even whenever I put them on today—they speak to me of God's desire for us to simply ask.

INQUIRING OF THE LORD

God is not only real, but personal and accessible. Because of this, we believe that we can ask Him anything and He will answer us. Moses marveled at this idea when he asked,

> *"What great nation ever had their gods as near to them as the Lord our God is near to us whenever we pray to him?"* (Deuteronomy 4:7 GWT)

In order to experience this kind of intimacy in prayer every day, we must learn to inquire of the Lord. To *inquire* basically means to ask Him questions. I have been asking the Lord questions for over forty years, and in all this time, I cannot think of a single question that He has failed to answer. I have had to learn how to inquire of Him.

> I cannot think of a single question that He has failed to answer.

There are many wonderful stories in the Bible that describe what happened when God's people began inquiring of Him. The Israelites would ask Him specific questions and get specific answers. For example, in Genesis 25 when Rebekah, the wife of Isaac, was having trouble conceiving, Isaac sought the Lord on his wife's behalf, and God answered his prayer. They were jubilant about becoming pregnant, but then something strange began to happen in her womb. It was as if the baby was thrashing about. So, she went to the Lord and inquired of Him, asking, *"If all is well, why am I like this?"*

The Lord responded to her immediately, telling her that she was having twins. God went on to tell Rebekah what His will was for each of her children:

"Two nations are in your womb, two peoples shall be separated from your body; one people shall be stronger than the other, and the older shall serve the younger." (Genesis 25:23)

The Bible goes on to say, *"So when her days were fulfilled for her to give birth, indeed there were twins in her womb"* (v. 24) Those twins were always in conflict. The children of Esau became the nation of the Edomites, who headed the list of the enemies of Israel for years, as mentioned in Psalm 83:5-8.

ASK HIM ANYTHING

When people expect the Lord to answer their questions, they soon start to ask Him anything. We see this is in the story of young Saul, who inquired of the Lord about his missing donkeys,

When they had come to the land of Zuph, Saul said to his servant who was with him, "Come, let us return, lest my father cease caring about the donkeys and become worried about us." And he said to him, "Look now, there is in this city a man of God, and he is an honorable man; all that he says surely comes to pass. So let us go there; perhaps he can show us the way that we should go." (1 Samuel 9:6)

Later in the story, when Saul himself was missing, the Israelites, *"inquired of the Lord further, 'Has the man come here yet?' And the Lord answered, 'There he is, hidden among the equipment'"* (1 Samuel 10:22).

THE LOST KEYS

I had taken a small group of men I had been discipling with me to preach. It turned out to be a great spiritual weekend, and as we were making our way home, we stopped at a diner for coffee along a barren stretch of highway in northern New York. But as it often does in this area, it began to snow. So, we cut the time short and headed back to the car only to find that we had been locked out. The driver anxiously patted himself down to find his keys while some of the men went back into the restaurant, crawling under the booths and asking the waitresses if they had seen them, but we all came up empty. It was getting darker and colder as the snow began to fall more rapidly, and we were still a long way from home. In a short time, several inches of snow had fallen, so we stomped all around the car, hoping to find the keys.

> We stomped all around the car, hoping to find the keys.

Finally, I gathered the men in a huddle and asked them to join me in prayer. I told them the Lord knew where the keys were and I believed He would tell us where to find them, if we asked believing. After a brief moment of expressing our hearts' gratitude for the good things that had happened that weekend, I asked the Lord to show us where the keys were. Immediately, He spoke to me saying, "They are in the garbage can." I relayed this to the men, and we ran toward the entrance of the restaurant where there was a large garbage barrel. We set the lid on the ground and emptied all the garbage out on it. When the keys did not appear, all the men looked to see my reaction. It was a tense moment. Then someone shook one of the coffee cups, and the keys came tumbling out. As it turned out, the driver had cleaned out the car when we first arrived, and inadvertently threw his keys into the barrel along with everything else. We all laughed, thanked the Lord, got back on the road, and headed for home. All we needed to do was ask Lord.

DAVID INQUIRED OF THE LORD

Perhaps no one in the Old Testament was more dependent on the Lord's input on life than David. He was so committed to acknowledging the Lord in all his ways that he wrote in Psalm 27:4:

One thing I have desired of the Lord, that will I seek: that I may dwell in the house of the Lord All the days of my life, to behold the beauty of the Lord, and to inquire in His temple.

Here are some other verses that show David asking specific questions and getting specific answers from the living Lord:

And he [the priest] inquired of the Lord for him [David], gave him provisions, and gave him the sword of Goliath the Philistine. (1 Samuel 22:10)

Therefore David inquired of the Lord, saying, "Shall I go and attack these Philistines?" And the Lord said to David, "Go and attack the Philistines, and save Keilah." (23:2)

So David inquired of the Lord, saying, "Shall I pursue this troop? Shall I overtake them?" And He answered him, "Pursue, for you shall surely overtake them and without fail recover all." (30:8)

It happened after this that David inquired of the Lord, saying, "Shall I go up to any of the cities of Judah?" And the Lord said to him, "Go up." David said, "Where shall I go up?" And He said, "To Hebron." (2 Samuel 2:1)

So David inquired of the Lord, saying, "Shall I go up against the Philistines? Will You deliver them into my hand?" And the Lord said to David, "Go up, for I will doubtless deliver the Philistines into your hand." (5:19)

Therefore David inquired of the Lord, and He said, "You shall not go up; circle around behind them, and come upon them in front of the mulberry trees." (v. 23)

> *Now there was a famine in the days of David for three years, year after year; and David inquired of the Lord. And the Lord answered, "It is because of Saul and his bloodthirsty house, because he killed the Gibeonites."* (21:1)

IT'S TIME TO SEEK THE LORD

The prophet Hosea spoke to the children of Israel, telling them it was time to seek the Lord:

> *Sow for yourselves righteousness; reap in mercy; break up your fallow ground, for it is time to seek the Lord, till He comes and rains righteousness on you.* (Hosea 10:12)

Seeking the Lord means taking time to hear from Him and gaining His perspective on the issues of our lives. Knowing His will has become even more necessary during these last days—which will be filled with social upheaval, dramatic change, and constant confusion.

Hosea also gave clues as to what seeking the Lord meant. It meant breaking up the fallow ground and sowing righteousness. Fallow ground describes a field that had once been fruitful, but then had been let go, neglected, or given a rest. When it was time to restore the field to usefulness, it would need to be cut down, cleaned up, and plowed again. Fallow ground can often be overrun with weeds or become stony. The hard ground needed to be broken up, turned over, and rocks needed to be removed once again. This would take time and effort.

Once the soil of our hearts has been broken up, it is time to sow new seed. Sowing is doing a bunch of little things repeatedly. You don't have to start by doing something big (like a forty-day fast). You can sow toward a long fasting period by fasting a bunch of little things at first. Some people think they need to do something radical, dramatic, or extreme to bring about the change they desire. You can try, but I have found that doing little things consistently is more effective than doing something dramatic all at once. Do the things you know are right like prayer, worship, giving, fasting, and meditating on God's Word. Putting seed in the ground means we need to expose our hearts to the Word of God.

When the Lord spoke to Israel through Hosea, inviting them to begin seeking Him again, He gave them a promise that He would respond to their efforts (acts of righteousness) by raining righteousness upon them. He promised that, after all the breaking, tilling, and sowing, they would reap His mercy.

There are a number of other promises found in the book of Hosea that help inspire us to seek the Lord afresh, trusting that He will respond. One of my personal favorites comes from Hosea 6:3:

Let us know, let us pursue the knowledge of the Lord. His going forth is established as the morning; He will come to us like the rain, like the latter and former rain to the earth.

My paraphrase of this verse is: "Let's learn all we can about the Lord. Let's press in to know Him, and He will respond to us as sure as the morning comes, and as certain as the rains of the spring and autumn which water the earth."

Hosea goes on to prophesy,

So you, by the help of your God, return; observe mercy and justice, and wait on your God continually. (12:6)

My paraphrase of this verse is: "Here is what you do: Turn to the Lord again, embrace both His mercy and judgment and wait continually before your God with expectation."

Then Hosea assured Israel that God will help them:

O Israel, you are destroyed, but your help is from Me. (13:9)

My paraphrase of this verse is: "You have brought this trouble upon yourself, but in Me is your help."

Then God promised healing:

I will heal your backsliding, I will love you freely, for My anger has been turned away from you. (14:4)

My paraphrase of this verse is: "For the Lord says, 'I will show them how to put an end to their spiritual regression and will demonstrate My love for them, proving to them that I am no longer angry for what they have done.'"

Finally, he gives them a powerful picture of spiritual growth:

"I will be like the dew to Israel; He shall grow like the lily, and lengthen his roots like Lebanon." (14:5)

My paraphrase of this verse is: "I will be like dew upon Israel and they shall look like a lily on the surface, but underneath will be roots like the cedars of Lebanon."

GOOD REASONS TO SEEK THE LORD

Hosea said it was time to seek God (see Hosea 10:12). How can you know it is time for you to seek the Lord?

- **When you feel holy discontentment:** One of the things that helps me know that it is time to seek the Lord is a thing I call *holy discontentment*. This is where I feel miserable, unsettled, restless, and longing for change. I used to think that being discontent was bad, but it depends on where it leads. If you find yourself standing with the fridge door open all the time, perhaps your inner hunger needs to be fulfilled, and you are looking for fulfillment in all the wrong places. If you feel like quitting your job, perhaps you should check to see if God isn't calling you into something that is tailor made for you. If you long to break free from where you are now, it's not time to take a cross-country motorcycle trip; perhaps it is the Lord stirring you up to go to another level. You will not know unless you ask Him. Discontentment can be a good thing, as long as it leads to seeking what God has for you.

- **When you are afraid:** If you feel afraid, this can be an indicator that it is time to seek the Lord. We can take all of our fears to Him, and ask Him what next steps we need to take:

  I sought the Lord, and He heard me, and delivered me from all my fears. They looked to Him and were radiant, and their faces were not ashamed. (Psalm 34:4-5)

- **When you need understanding:** Whenever we need to know what is happening, it should be our response to seek the Lord:

  Those who seek the Lord understand all. (Proverbs 28:5)

- **When you need provision:** Jesus told us to ask for our daily bread, as if it were a normal part of our relationship with our heavenly Father.

  The young lions lack and suffer hunger; But those who seek the Lord shall not lack any good thing. (Psalm 34:10)

- **When it is difficult to discern what is happening:** Another story that is especially interesting, because of the way it illustrates how things went wrong when the Children of Israel failed to seek the Lord, can be found in Joshua 9. The inhabitants of Gibeon heard that God had destroyed Jericho and that they were next on the list, so they went to see if the Israelites would make a covenant with them. They pretended to have come from a far country instead of being one of the local tribes that Israel was to displace and destroy. They put on old clothes and old sandals, carried old wine skins, and had old moldy bread on hand to give the impression that they had been on a long journey. It says in Joshua 9:14, that the leaders of Israel, "did not ask counsel of the Lord." So, the Israelites were deceived into making a covenant with a people that they were supposed to eliminate. This reflected badly on their leadership (Joshua 9:18).

- **When things go wrong:** Another example of a time to seek the Lord was when the Children of Israel were defeated at the battle for Ai. It was a city they should have easily won, so their *loss was deeply discouraging. The Israelites went back to the Lord and inquired of Him as to why they* had been defeated. Joshua tore his clothes and fell down on his face before the *ark of the Lord until evening.* God began a process of narrowing it down from two and a half million people to one man named Achan who had sinned. The Lord could have just given his name, but He took them through the process of hearing from Him (see Joshua 7:1–26).

- **When you need direction:** Another time, in Judges 20:18, the Children of Israel inquired of the Lord, asking for specific direction. He gave them a specific answer:

Then the children of Israel arose and went up to the house of God to inquire of God. They said, "Which of us shall go up first to battle against the children of Benjamin?" The Lord said, "Judah first!"

In Addendum Two in the back of this book, I have included a list of promises that will help build assurance during times when you are seeking the Lord.

HOW TO SEEK THE LORD?

Men of old, when surrounded by menacing armies, would often stop and inquire of the Lord, asking for His perspective during the "fog of war." They sought His help in order to know what to do. Hearing from Him during our own conflicts will sustain our hearts when our heads are not sure what to do. Seeking the Lord is the only way I know to endure my many problems with poise, purpose, and peace.

Seeking and searching for the Lord's will is a lifelong pursuit. It should become part of our great quest in life. When the Lord used Hosea to help move the people from a fallow time to a fruitful time, He told them to begin by seeking Him. Here are some practical things you can do now:

- **Be of good cheer:** Jesus said this about six times to people who needed His help. I cannot help but think He was saying this because He knows that having the right attitude can help our receptivity. It is like putting our antenna up to receive from God. We all know that being anxious or stressed or fearful are counterproductive when trying to hear from the Lord. Gratitude is the key that opens up everything.

- **Get quiet:** Being still, slowing our minds down, and shutting down distractions are basic tools that help us as we seek the Lord to receive the direction we need. He will not compete with the noise and distractions that often fill our lives.

- **Look to Jesus:** Seeking the Lord also means looking toward the Lord, which involves taking our eyes off of what others are doing. As we look to Jesus, we should ask, "What would He say to me, right now?" We also need to take our eyes off our circumstances, no matter what they are say, and no matter how awful things look to our natural eyes. Keep your eyes on Jesus.

- **Become childlike:** The goal is to keep our childlike trust. This is evident by the way we ask Him questions. As a new believer, I came to the conclusion that Jesus was not rude. If I asked Him a question, He would always answer me.

HE WILL RESPOND

When Jesus taught us in Matthew 7:7-8 to seek the Lord, He said we would find. Notice how emphatic He was.

Usually, when it is time to seek the Lord, we are coming from a place where we feel the need to start over, or are recovering from a fallen spiritual condition, rather than coming from a position of strength. This can make it difficult for us to believe that God will respond.

In Jeremiah 29:11-13, when the Lord invited the Children of Israel to come back to Him, they were reluctant because they did not feel like He would respond favorably. He assured them that He was *for them*, not *against them*. He wanted to give them a hope and a future.

> *"When you know how much I think about you and how good my intentions are toward you, you will pray to Me, and I will listen to you. And you will find Me when you seek Me with all your heart."*

Notice how after He assures them of His heart for them, it leads to their being able to pray and seek the Lord.

He doesn't tell us to seek Him without giving us the incentive to do it. We need to resolve to do it with all our hearts, saying, "I not coming up for air until I have what I am looking for."

KNOCKING

I am full of ideas, vision, and action. I like seeing things happen and am not afraid of trying new things or taking risks. This has led to a very fulfilling life with lots of accomplishments to show for it, but it took me a while to gain the confidence to trust what was going on inside of me and begin to learn how to be guided by desires and inner promptings. I was not always this brave.

As a young disciple, I was full of ideas but afraid to try anything that the Lord hadn't told me to do. This caused me to be hesitant, always living in a crouch, thinking I might miss the Lord. When I asked Him about this, He spoke to me, saying that He did not mind my trying things or exploring ideas, as long as I had the humility to admit that it was not His leading as soon as I realized it. I would

He did not mind my trying things or exploring ideas.

have to have the humility to back out and go back to seeking Him. He wanted me to walk before Him in such a way that, if He asked me to let go of something, I would. He did not want me to be like the horse that needed a bit and bridle before I would do anything; instead, He wanted me to become sensitive to the slightest touch of His reins, directing me as He willed.

This freed me up to try things to test and see if He was in it or not. Again, it is all in abiding (see John 15:7). If we abide in Him, which means living in communion with Him, and letting His Word abide in us, so that our lives are ordered by biblical precedents and principles, and if we abide in His love, we can do what we will, and it is as if it was Him leading us.

David told Nathan the prophet that he wanted to build God a house. Nathan's response was, *"Do what is in your heart for God is with you"* (2 Samuel 7:3). He knew David was a man after God's own heart, but the prophet hadn't even gotten down the hallway when the Lord spoke to Him, telling him to go back and tell David that he was not to build Him a house, but that his son would do it.

There is a place for doing what is in your heart, trusting that, if it is not right, the Lord will talk with you about it. Because of our relationship with Him, we can rest in the fact that, if it were not so, the Lord would tell us. Jesus said something along this line in John 14:2:

In My Father's house are many mansions; if it were not so, I would have told you. I go to prepare a place for you.

Notice that He said, *"If it were not so, I would have told you."* This is an amazing fact that applies to many things, including guidance. If you are doing something wrong, believing something wrong, or going in the wrong direction, He will tell you. This comes out of our "abiding in Him and He in us" kind of relationship, which means we must cultivate a sensitivity to His voice through obedience and responsiveness. If you are not abiding in Him, you may not recognize His doing this at the time.

Some people refuse to go forward until they have all the guidance they need up front. For me, it rarely happens this way. Most of my direction unfolds as I go, walking with an open heart, trying to be sensitive and deferential to Him. He does not want me to be like a horse that has to be prodded or made to move:

Do not be like the horse or like the mule, which have no understanding, which must be harnessed with bit and bridle, else they will not come near you. (Psalm 32:9)

What Jesus said about our knocking has been especially helpful to me through the years. It not only gave me permission to test to see if what I am feeling as direction was the Lord's will by prayerfully "knocking," but it contained a powerful promise that something would happen as a result of my seeking the Lord.

Most of my direction unfolds as I go, walking with an open heart, trying to be sensitive and deferential to Him.

THREE WORDS THAT CHANGED EVERYTHING

We had moved to New York from Canada so I could pastor a church that was being planted there. To make the transition complete, I had to find a house for my young family. I had looked at all kinds of places, mostly old fixer-uppers, which were all we thought we could afford at that time. However, as we looked closer into it, we realized that many of these needed too much work or had suddenly become overpriced because of a housing boom that hit our small town as a result of the expansion of a nearby military base.

At any rate, we looked for three months and still could not find anything. I had been asking God to guide us in general but had not seriously gotten down to asking Him questions about our search. From my first question, He showed me what I had been doing wrong. He spoke to me immediately, saying, "Look for land." The idea of looking for land had crossed my mind numerous times before, but it implied building a house, which I did not think we had the time or money to do. I protested the idea aloud in prayer, saying that our church was growing and needed all my time. Plus, a new house seemed out of reach for us. Yet, I knew He had spoken.

Well, I got off my knees and went out looking for land. Before long, I ended up in an area that I was not familiar with and met a man from our church. When I told him that I was out looking for land, his face lit up, and he told me that he had just the thing. He took me to a beautiful meadow, which was surrounded by mature trees. It felt secluded but was only a mile from a good school and not that far from the church. We began the process of buying the property that very day. With our money still in Canada, from the sale of our house there, we bought a log-home kit and had it shipped across the border, saving a huge loss by not exchanging our money to US funds. Before long, we had a lovely new house for less than it would have cost us to restore an old one. I had searched for three months and came up empty, but everything took a different direction on the day that I got a word from the Lord.

SOME THINGS I HAVE LEARNED

As a new believer, I began seeking the Lord and asking Him questions. I had to learn the lesson of not limiting Him as to *how* or *when* He should answer. I found out early that He rarely answers the same way twice (see Hebrews 1:1). I think He does this so that we don't become dependent upon formulas or seek out methods, but truly become dependent upon Him. There is something in our nature that likes formulas and routine, but He wants a relationship with us.

If the Lord uses a certain book to speak to me, my tendency is to go out and get every other book the author wrote. If He uses a prophet to speak to me, then I tend to look to that prophet the next time I need help. If He uses a radio

---

There is something in our nature that likes formulas and routine, but He wants a relationship with us.

preacher, then when I get in the car, I automatically tune the dial to that station. I have had to learn that, once I shared my questions with Him, I had to let Him choose the method He wanted to use to speak. He wants me to seek Him, not the means He uses to speak to me. Once I learned that, the answer always came through. In fact, He has never failed to answer a single question that I have asked Him in all these years.

The Lord speaks in different ways at different times (see Hebrews 1:1) He can use any number of means to get through to us, including:

- the Scriptures
- sermons and testimonies
- wise counsel
- books and media
- the prayers of others
- prophecy and visions

I also learned not to tell Him when to answer or how. I stay clear of the *why* questions as well.

A good place to begin is by getting a notebook and itemizing the things you need answers for, listing all the areas where you need a breakthrough. Sometimes, I write out my questions, just to sort out what I really need, getting to the heart of the matter. I call this *praying on paper*. David called his notebook, *the Psalms of David*.

I have learned that, when I am reluctant to talk things over with Him, it is usually because I don't trust Him, or I want my way more than I want His. The fact is we will have to seek the Lord, either when we are making our plans or in the end when we need His help to get out of the mess we have created. Either way, we need to pray.

When I first bring my heart before Him, I tend to see the things that make me feel disqualified to be close to Him or to hear from Him, but I have learned that these are like the dust particles in the air; they are there all the time, but we only see them because of the sunlight coming in the room at the right time, from the right angle. We only see our faults and failures because we are in His presence. Now I know to simply acknowledge what I see, ask for cleansing, and move on. If I don't, I will not get anywhere in prayer.

I am often tempted to get up as soon as I hear from Him, but sometimes the best part comes when I linger a little longer before the Lord, flushing my heart's affection for Him.

I will set a predetermined timeframe on how long to seek the Lord,

> I have learned that, when I am reluctant to talk things over with Him, it is usually because I want my way more than I want His.

depending on the issue. This is not intended to limit God, but it helps motivate me to stay focused about the issue at hand.

I usually begin with a prolonged time of praying in tongues. I think this is one of the fastest means of getting past my head and letting His Spirit pray through my spirit. He often speaks to me through the openness of heart that this kind of praying creates.

Before I begin, I try to consider what my desired outcome should be. I try not to lose sight of this, no matter where the process leads. Sometimes, the route He takes seems disconnected to what I am praying about, but it often leads to the root of the problem.

If I shut myself away for a couple of days on a personal retreat, I will sometimes begin by taking a nap in His presence. This may seem like a waste of time, but He does not mind it. When I take our pastors' retreat each fall, I encourage each of the men to spend the first day just resting in His presence, with no pressure to hear from Him that first day at all. It is not a write-off. It is difficult to be spiritual and exhausted at the same time.

When I am praying and seeking the Lord, I begin by telling Him what I am thinking about a certain area, as if He didn't know. I know that He knows, but I don't get the benefit of having to express myself if I pray like He knows. Just hearing myself say things out loud helps a great deal.

I always want Him to "download" the whole thing to me at once, but He tends to dole it out in small pieces over time. He does not want to be a guidance dispenser; He wants to be my companion and Lord.

I tend to get more out of these times aside if I fast something. You can fast things as well as food. I have given up television, newspapers, or other things that I enjoy just to focus on what is really important. Again, this is more for my benefit, as it causes me to be more focused and intentional.

I will ask Him to confirm what He has been saying to me through the counsel of godly people.

I don't over-spiritualize things. I don't fast and pray about whether or not to buy peas or beans. I only bring the things before Him that I truly need His perspective on.

It is like being in one of those corn mazes. You have to find your way out of a maze made of twelve-feet-tall corn that has been cut into a puzzle of paths. You enter one end of the field and try to find your way out of the other end. If you get lost, you can speak into a corrugated pipe, and someone who is in a tower overlooking the maze, can hear you, see you, and give you the direction you need to keep moving. Sounds like prayer, right? In this case, as it is when we are seeking the Lord, perspective is everything.

At the Ripley's "Believe It or Not" Museum in Niagara Falls, Ontario, there once stood a fiberglass cast of the world's tallest man, Robert Wadlow. He was almost nine feet tall. Actually, it was only half of the cast of Robert, because the back half was open, with a small staircase going up his back. You could climb up the stairs and look out through his eyes. Everything looked different from that perspective. In the same way, God invites us to look at our lives, our circumstances, even our future, through His eyes. His perspective changes everything. Wisdom is His perspective.

ASSIGNMENTS

The big difference between David and Saul was in their willfulness. David remained very childlike, totally yielded to the Lord for everything, whereas Saul became more self-willed, doing whatever he wanted to do. Then, when he tried to inquire of the Lord, Saul was ignored.

> *And when Saul inquired of the Lord, the Lord did not answer him, either by dreams or by Urim or by the prophets.* (1 Samuel 28:6)

Saul became so desperate for direction that he sought it from the devil, by going to a fortune teller. The summary of Saul's life reads like this:

> *So Saul died for his unfaithfulness which he had committed against the Lord, because he did not keep the word of the Lord, and also because he consulted a medium for guidance. But he did not inquire of the Lord; therefore He killed him, and turned the kingdom over to David the son of Jesse.* (1 Chronicles 10:13-14)

PART SIX: FIGHTING FOR THE WILL OF GOD

The apostle Paul had written to the Christians at Ephesus, urging them to become more detached from this life and apply themselves to understanding what the will of God is:

See then that you walk circumspectly, not as fools but as wise, redeeming the time, because the days are evil. Therefore, do not be unwise, but understand what the will of the Lord is. (5:15–17)

Just as in Paul's day, we need wisdom to know what the will of God is. Let's begin by looking for a practical definition for the will of God, moving from the broadest sense of the word to how we can apply it to our everyday lives.

One of the essential things we need to understand about God's will is that it is not something that comes automatically or that we have by default, but something we must insist upon in prayer. It needs to be sought after and sometimes even fought for. Some believers coast along, hoping they will stumble into the will of God, or worse, they bulldoze their way through everything to bring about the will of God

Many Christians conclude that everything that happens to them is the will of God. They conclude, if it happened, God must have allowed it. This is more of a Muslim mindset than Christian. Muslims believe that everything that happens is somehow the will of Allah.

Consider this in light of the prayer efforts of Epaphras, who was always interceding for the members of his church at Colossi as he sat in prison with Paul:

Always laboring fervently for you in prayers, that you may stand perfect and complete in all the will of God. (Colossians 4:12)

Paul could hear Epaphras praying, striving, and wrestling in prayer for his church. Paul could hear his heart. Epaphras had an invested interest in Colossi and the other two churches nearby. Perhaps he was the one who helped start them. According to his actions, he believed that, unless he wrestled in prayer for the churches, they would not come into the will of God.

It is obvious that both Epaphras and Paul believed that, unless they prayed for God's will to come, it would not happen. God's will must be prayed, procured, or pronounced into being, or it will not happen.

What are you fighting for? Are you fighting for your church, or with your church? Are you fighting for your pastor, that God would guide him, or are you fighting against him? Who are you fighting for? What are you laboring in prayer for? Your family? Nobody is going to pray for your family like you. Your pastor won't. Your best friend won't. Where is your invested interest?

God's will must be prayed, procured, or pronounced into being, or it will not happen.

Who was Epaphras fighting with? I don't think he had to force God's hand to act, nor did he seem all that focused on the devil. At least there is no mention of this. I do know that, in my own life, the biggest contender for the will of God is my own will, base desires, and passivity.

THE BATTLE FOR OUR WILL

Because we are created in the image of God, we are also given a free will. Our will is the strongest thing in all the universe because God will not break it, the devil cannot break it, and nobody else can make us do what we don't want to do. This is why there is such a battle to see to whom we will yield our wills.

When our flesh dominates our wills, it is called being self-willed. When our flesh is in control, it puts us at odds with doing those things that please God. There are many verses warning us not to become self-willed.

When the devil dominates our wills, making us do what he wants, it is called demonic possession. The enemy's goal is to get us to yield our wills to him, even if he has to seduce us, deceive us, or dominate us to do it—anything so that we will do his bidding. The more he can work through us, the more damage he can do in other people's lives.

In fact, the devil's primary purpose behind drawing people into the abuse of drugs and alcohol in our society today is to effectively neutralize their wills, weaken them, put them out of gear—anything so he can make them more yielded to his purposes. People do things under the influence of drugs and alcohol that they are shocked to read about in the newspapers afterward. In fact, many deny doing what they've done because it is not their nature to do such things when they are sober.

Something else we have to contend with is surrendering to the will of others. People often want us to yield our wills to theirs. They do this through manipulation, control, and legalism—anything to get us to conform to their wills, which are driven by their own flesh and selfish-ambition.

God's desire is that we would choose to submit our wills to His, becoming like a hand in a glove, so that we can work together as one. This combination is unbeatable. To do this, He inspires us to surrender our wills to His, but He never forces us to do anything.

> The enemy's goal is to get us to yield our wills to him.

ENDURING TO RECEIVE

We cannot just sit around waiting for what God has showed us to fulfill itself. Our job, so to speak, is to bring what He has promised into being. We often have to endure circumstances that seem to be just the opposite of what He has shown us to be His will. Listen to the tone of these scriptures given by the writer of Hebrews. They show us our need or responsibility to endure in order to come into what God has in His heart for us:

And we desire that each one of you show the same diligence to the full assurance of hope until the end, that you do not become sluggish, but imitate those who through faith and patience inherit the promises. For when God made a promise to Abraham, because He could swear by no one greater, He swore by Himself, saying, "Surely blessing I will bless you, and multiplying I will multiply you. And so, after he had patiently endured, he obtained the promise." (6:11-15)

Let us hold fast the confession of our hope without wavering, for He who promised is faithful. (10:23)

A RESOLUTION

Around the beginning of each New Year, people often take time to reflect on where they have been and where they are going in the coming year. Some people also use this time to make resolutions, hoping to improve their lives. Most of us want to live more balanced lives, to learn to say "no" so we can spend our time and money more wisely, to improve our relationships, and to get a better handle on what we do, say, and eat. The list can go on and on because it is easy to see where we need improvement. The difficult part is keeping these resolutions.

May I suggest something simpler? If you are going to make any resolution which will truly change your life, then why not limit it to just one resolution: Let's choose to please the Lord in all of our choices, big and small. Then, as a result, we will walk in more of His love, which is what often leads to our discovering what His purpose is for our lives. These two things are wrapped up in pleasing Him. Let's make this resolution again and again.

Here are some ways in which we can begin this quest:

- **Put others ahead of ourselves:**

    Let nothing be done through selfish ambition or conceit, but in lowliness of mind let each esteem others better than himself. (Philippians 2:3)

- **Live to the benefit of others:**

    Not seeking my own profit, but the profit of many, that they may be saved. (1 Corinthians 10:33)

- **Choose those things that please Him:**

    For thus says the Lord: "To the eunuchs who keep My Sabbaths, and choose what pleases Me, and hold fast My covenant, even to them I will give in My house and within My walls a place and a name better than that of sons and daughters; I will give them an everlasting name that shall not be cut off." (Isaiah 56:4-5)

There are some basic things on the surface of God's Word that tell us what His will is. For example, some people develop relationships with others that lead them into sin. This cannot be God's will:

For this is the will of God, your sanctification: that you should abstain from sexual immorality; that each of you should know how to possess his own vessel in sanctification and honor, not in passion of lust, like the Gentiles who do not know God; that no one should take advantage of and defraud his brother in this matter, because the Lord is the avenger of all such, as we also forewarned you and testified. (1 Thessalonians 4:3-6)

LIVING BELOW OUR GOD-GIVEN POTENTIAL

One day, as I drove passed the house of my neighbor, I noticed that he was mowing a little patch of lawn with a great big John Deere tractor. At first, I laughed at the sight, as I thought, *That thing was made for something more.* Then, it hit me. This is like so many Christians, living beneath their potential because they never find out what God created for them to do. They are just going around in circles, without accomplishing anything. I could imagine God watching them, saying to Himself, "You were made for much more than this."

This is true of a lot of people. I suspect the reason we live below our potential is we do not press in for the will of God for our lives.

ASSIGNMENTS

- This list of things God delights in is not complete. There are other verses that reveal what God delights in. Try to find them.

- What brings you this kind of pleasure at a heart level? I don't mean things you enjoy, but things that bring real heart satisfaction. Again, delight is the highest form of pleasure. I bet you can't name three things that truly delight your heart. Write them out and see for yourself.

- There are things found in Scripture that have long delighted the hearts of people in the Bible. See if you can find them.

PART SEVEN: DISCERNING GOD'S VOICE

To be successful in our great quest, and to come into God's immediate will and purpose, we must learn to hear His voice. This is a lifelong quest in itself as it will take a lifetime to learn. I am better at doing it now than when I first started out, but I am still learning.

Learning to hear from Jesus regularly is perhaps one of the greatest things we can experience in this life. He said, *"My sheep hear My voice"* (John 10:27). This not only shows that it's possible, but it should be normal and central to our relationship with Him.

Many Christians are not confident in saying that they have heard from Him, while others think He tells them whether to buy beans or peas. Somewhere in the middle of these two extremes, I believe we can find Him speaking, even as a Father longs to communicate His heart to His children. While I don't believe He speaks to us about every little detail all the time, we should know the wonder of hearing His voice as an integral part of being in fellowship with Him. Because I believe He is a real person and that He isn't rude, if I ask Him a question, He will answer me. Our being able to talk to Him directly and have Him answer is the one factor that makes Christianity distinct from every other religion known to man. In this Study Guide, we will give a significant amount of space to learning about how to hear His voice.

The writer of Hebrews wrote:

God, who at various times and in various ways spoke in time past.... (1:1)

In other words, the Lord doesn't always use the same way to speak to us each time. Hearing from God does not come naturally but is a skill that is gained by having an intimate relationship with the Lord. In this study, I have listed some principles that have helped me along the way, but this is not an attempt to create a method to hear from God. The Lord does not want to be like a vending machine, where we put something in and, automatically, get something out. We need to learn to put our trust in Him rather than in a method.

> **The Lord does not want to be like a vending machine, where we put something in and, automatically, get something out.**

Let's review a concept I taught on earlier: God can use the radio, Scripture, another believer, a sermon, or even an idea that comes into your mind. God uses many ways, even though we are creatures of habit. We turn on the radio in the car, and God speaks to us through the radio preacher. So, the next time we need to hear from God, we go out to the car and scan for a station until we find something. God says, "Oh, no! That was not the radio. That was Me."

You read a book, and God speaks to you through it so that, the next time you need to hear from God, you go out and buy every book written by the author of that book. "It's not the man, it's ME! I know when you stand, I know when you sit, and I know what you need," God says.

Hebrews 1:1 says that He speaks in different ways at different times. We need to hear from God. It's not just something that would be nice once in a while; it is critical that we hear from Him. If not, we will settle for the wrong voice.

During the filming of the animated film, *The Prince of Egypt*, Steven Spielberg was discussing with his staff the scene where God speaks to Moses out of the burning bush. The actor who supplied the voice of young Moses was Val Kilmer. The producers and writers suggested getting someone with a deep, authoritative voice like Charlton Heston or James Earl Jones to be the voice of God. Finally, Spielberg brushed all this aside by saying, "No, we must use Val Kilmer's voice because, when God speaks to us, He always uses our own voice."[6]

The reason we need to learn to discern the voice of God is just that. When God speaks to us, He uses our own voices. We don't usually hear the actual voice of God. Women don't hear an authoritative male voice; He uses their voice. He also uses our vernacular, colloquialism, and mental faculties.

For that matter, the devil uses our own voice as well. We don't actually hear him speaking when he tempts us; we hear our voices speaking his thoughts. For that matter, our flesh and our spirits also use our own voices, as do our souls. This is known as our "inner dialogue." We can hear all of these voices at work within us at different times.

In other words, the Lord doesn't tend to use the same way to speak to us each time. This factor alone is intended to help us learn to trust in Him rather than in a method. Hearing from God does not come naturally, but is a skill that is gained over time by having an intimate relationship with the Lord.

> **When God speaks to us, He uses our own voices.**

THE VOICE OF ANOTHER

Jesus warned us about listening to the voice of another in John 10:1-6:

> *Most assuredly, I say to you, he who does no enter the sheepfold by the door, but climbs up some other way, the same is a thief and a robber. But he who enters by the door is the shepherd of the sheep. To him the doorkeeper opens, and the sheep hear his voice; and he calls his own sheep by name and leads them out. And when he brings out his own sheep, he goes before them; and the sheep follow him, for they know his voice. Yet they will by no means follow a stranger, but will flee from him, for they do not know the voice of strangers.*

We must learn to respond to the Shepherd's voice. If we don't, we will become prone to follow another's voice. This other voice is a non-shepherding voice, which is the voice of a thief. What does he steal from us?

- our peace of mind
- our sense of security

- our confidence
- our standing in Christ

Learning to recognize the Shepherd's voice involves more than listening to see if what is said is scriptural or not. Our flesh can use scripture. So can the devil, for that matter. One sure way to judge whether it is Him speaking to us or not is by the effect it has on our hearts. Our own ideas cannot produce the same effect that His voice does. For example, His voice leaves us with a peace that surpasses our understanding. If we could produce this kind of peace, we would produce it all the time. Like hospital patients who are given a pump to medicate themselves, we would be pumping peace and joy into our hearts all the time. We can't, or we would. However, His words can and do.

All our belief cannot produce the kind of faith that a *rhema* produces. *"Faith comes by hearing, and hearing by the word [rhema] of God"* (Romans 10:17). When He speaks, His words contain faith that comes into our hearts.

Words are like buckets that contain what is uppermost in our hearts. Someone with a sweet heart will speak sweet words. Bitter hearts speak bitter words. Deceitful hearts speak deceitful words. A heart full of faith tends to call those things that are not as though they were. Whatever is in abundance in our hearts, our mouths speak.

Words that flow from God's heart contain faith, joy, peace, and hope. When He speaks to us, His words leave these effects on our hearts. We will feel faith rise within us. We will feel beloved or have a deep sense of peace or hope for the future. Jesus was talking about this when He said that out of the abundance of our hearts, our mouths speak. This is not only true of our hearts, but also of God's heart. His words are saturated with what is in His heart.

You can tell what any voice you are listening to—whether it is in your own heart, through another speaking in a sermon, in a book, in friendships or counseling, or in the spirit realm—by the effect it has on you. Words, like buckets, contain whatever is in the heart of the person who speaks them. This is also true of the devil's words. His words are incapable of producing faith, joy, peace, or grace, because he does not have any of these things in his heart. Instead, his heart is full of fear, condemnation, rejection, and bitterness, and his words taint everything he says. We know it is him speaking by the effect of his words.

What is the abundance of the devil's heart? Fear. He is very afraid and the father of the original fear. He is condemned already and knows his fate. He is deceived and a deceiver and is the father of lies. He has no hope or prospect of change.

Jesus told us to judge the fruit of a prophet. The word *fruit* is the *effect* of the words or what the words produces. You can tell who is speaking, God or the devil, by the effect their words produce in your heart or in the atmosphere of a meeting. We need to learn to judge the effect more than the words themselves. The words may have some truth in them, but are they life-giving?

THE VOICE OF OUR FLESH

The voice of our souls is our logic or reason, which can be at odds with the voice of our spirits.

The voice of our flesh usually speaks first and the loudest. It is bold and insistent. We can discern this voice by the fact that it is only selfish. It is self-preserving, self-serving, self-aggrandizing, and self-pleasing. We really need to learn to recognize the voice of our flesh because it speaks to us much more often than the devil. Once we master this, we will be in a better position to discern when other people's flesh is trying to speak into our lives.

If we wait, our spirits, where Christ lives, will speak. That voice is usually quieter.

The technical term for the voice of our spirits is *conscience*. If we listen to it, we will not go wrong.

Our spirits and our flesh are in constant conflict. Our souls can see the desires of both entities and hear the voices of both.

While I was preparing for my first mission trip to India, I spent a week on an island in the South China Sea, getting adjusted to another culture and recovering from jet-lag. One day, as I was walking through the old fishing village, I stopped at a little store that was filled with all kinds of unusual things. As I entered, I walked past the lady at the cash register and walked slowly around the tables that were covered with antiques, carvings, and unusual objects. When I got to the back of the store, I saw a wallet among the clutter. It was a new wallet filled with money. In fact, it had so much money in it that it looked like a hamburger. I could see the bills sticking out of the sides all around the wallet.

Right away, my flesh spoke up and said, "Pick it up and keep walking. No one will know that it is not yours." This voice shocked me a bit.

As I waited, my spirit quietly spoke, saying firmly, "We don't live that way."

My flesh said, "But no one knows you on this island. You can casually walk out with it and no one will know the difference."

I waited, and my spirit spoke, "God is looking, and He knows."

My flesh became even more adamant, "Just take it, you could use the money."

As I waited, my spirit spoke, "What would you want someone to do if they found your wallet?"

> **The voice of our flesh usually speaks first and the loudest.**

I knew that I should do unto others as I would have them do unto me, but my flesh countered this with, "You don't have enough money for this trip. Besides, you can give it to the poor. Pick it up and walk out." I picked it up and walked to the front of the store, where I handed it to the cashier.

As I stepped outside, I felt so good. I like myself whenever I win these battles. Then I chuckled to myself as I realized that I had now created the same kind of war in the cashier's heart, but I was free. The point is none of this battle had anything to do with the devil or the Holy Spirit. It was all within me.

LISTENING TO THE WRONG VOICE

Like background music in a store, which we hear but are not always aware of, there are many voices playing in the background of our lives all the time. In fact, there are many kinds of voices going through the room you are sitting in right now. If you had the right receiver, you could listen to those voices. They are radio voices, television voices, and telephone voices—many kinds of voices.

What is true in the natural is just as true in the spiritual realm. There are many kinds of voices in this world. Evil spirits speak to us all the time, as do angels. Our flesh is constantly speaking, other people's flesh is speaking to us, the Holy Spirit speaks, and our spirits speak to us regularly. Knowing how to discern between these voices is key.

If you listen to the wrong voice, it can separate you from God.

If you listen to the wrong voice, it can separate you from God. As a pastor, I have seen this happen many times. People hear condemnation, they hear rejection, and they hear blame, all of which tends to separate them from the One who really cares about them. You can see this at work in the story of Elijah when he was staying with the hospitable family. For some reason, their young son died. The Bible does not say how or why, but it does show the first thing that came out of the mother's mouth:

> *So she said to Elijah, "What have I to do with you, O man of God? Have you come to me to bring my sin to remembrance, and to kill my son?"*
> (1 Kings 17:18)

A paraphrase of this verse says, "Why are you in my house? Did you come to reveal my sins and bring the judgment of God on me?"

She was listening to the wrong voice.

Even today, the first thing that happens when people become sick or have an accident is that they blame God, concluding that He let it happen because He doesn't like them anymore or perhaps because they didn't pray enough that day. As soon as difficulties come in our lives, the wrong voice comes right along behind it trying to put a wedge between us and God.

The voice of the enemy does not come only in the form of temptation, but more incessantly, in the voice of condemnation, accusation, slander, fear, and worry—anything to get you to act accordingly.

Listening to the wrong voice can:

- **Separate us from God,** which causes us to want to avoid spending time with Someone whom we believe has hurt us in the past, rejects us now, or is out to ruin our future.

- **Create debilitating fear**, which causes us to live our lives now according to the "what if" of something we fear might happen someday.

- **Create condemnation**, which causes us to sense that we are living under the disapproving gaze of God.

- **Lead to spiritual extremes**, which cause us to swing between legalism or looseness.

- **Lead to pride**, which is where we get a distorted view of ourselves.

- **Cause us to reject God because we think He has rejected us**. Rejection always begets rejection.

- **Create doubts**. When people blame God for all their problems, they are listening to the wrong voice.

- **Create depression**, which is what happens whenever we impose the past on the future.

- **Cause all kinds of divisions**, which is why we remove ourselves from the Body of Christ, thus separating ourselves from the grace of God.

You can tell what you are listening to by what comes out of your mouth. Our mouths will always speak what is on the top of our hearts. Jesus said that, out of the abundance of our hearts, our mouths speak (Matthew 12:34-35). We are influenced by whatever voice we are most receptive to—either the sounds of darkness of the melodies of heaven.

THE MELODIES OF HEAVEN

God knows the future, because He wrote it, so He always speaks hope. Things are going to get better and brighter, and things will always turn out for our good. Jesus is the Prince of Peace, so His words contain a peace that doesn't make sense when our circumstances are confusing. He is love, so He does not use fear to speak to us. These two things are mutually exclusive and cannot exist in the same place at the same time. He cannot be condemning us and praying for us at the same time. Who is he that is against us? Not God, He is for us and wants us to overcome.

If we could go to heaven for a minute or two, we would be amazed at how positive the place is—how peacefully positive it is there. While we cannot escape to heaven every time things become tense here, we can tune our ears to the melodies of heaven. When we do, this is what we will hear:

- **He is the God of never-ending encouragement:**

    Now may our Lord Jesus Christ Himself, and our God and Father, who has loved us and given us everlasting consolation and good hope by grace, comfort your hearts and establish you in every good word and work. (2 Thessalonians 2:16-17)

    The term *everlasting consolation and good hope*, has been rendered as "unending encouragement and unfailing hope," in the J. B. Phillips translation, which over the years has proven to be a more useful phrase to me as so often I have had heard the voices of discouragement try to dissuade me from being a visionary leader in the church. I have had to draw from the never-ending encouragement that He has made available.

- **He is the God of all comfort:**

    Blessed be the God and Father of our Lord Jesus Christ, the Father of mercies and God of all comfort, who comforts us in all our tribulation, that we may be able to comfort those who are in any trouble, with the comfort with which we ourselves are comforted by God. (2 Corinthians 1:3-4)

    The term *God of all comfort* involves calling us near to Himself, filling our hearts with assurance of His love, and giving us the perspective we need to help us calmly face any situation that would otherwise overwhelm us.

- **He is the God of all hope:**

    Now may the God of hope fill you with all joy and peace in believing, that you may abound in hope by the power of the Holy Spirit. (Romans 15:13)

    Hope is one of the most valuable commodities in the world today. This becomes even more apparent if you have been among a people who have none. To them, there is no visible prospect of change, no way out, and no chance of things getting better. There is always life on the other side of whatever you are presently going through. Whatever you are presently going through will not last, if you keep your heart in hope.

When we learn to know the voice of the Spirit, we find that it is largely made up of edification, exhortation, and comfort (1 Corinthians 14:3).

If you are not aware of your hunger for the Lord or the things of God, I suggest you abstain for a while from all the other voices in your life. Shut off the radio, turn off the music, let the tube grow cold, and then your spiritual hunger will come back.

I remember being impacted by a prophecy when I was a new Christian, which said that God will not compete with all the other noise in the world. If we turned it off and would come aside from the din all around us, we would hear from Him. Yet, if we preferred to listen to all the other voices in our lives, He would not compete with them; instead, He would withdraw until we sought to hear from Him.

HIS WORDS ALWAYS PRODUCE LIFE

Listening to the right voice always produces fruit, life, and fellowship. Jesus said in John 15:7-8,

If you abide in Me, and My words abide in you, you will ask what you desire, and it shall be done for you. By this My Father is glorified, that you bear much fruit; so you will be My disciples.

His words are not just what we read in the Bible, but what He is saying to us in our hearts, or in sermons, or in prophecy, or when He quickens scriptures to us. It is not so much what He said, but what He is saying that produces fruit in us.

Imagine growing up having only heard the voices of the Pharisees. Their voices were condemning, accusatory, filled with contradictions and restrictions. What they had to say complicated the spiritual lives of the people. All the while, what they said made God look petty, mean, and vindictive. God was thought to be as austere and joyless as the Pharisees were themselves. Then, all of a sudden, you hear Jesus talking about who God the Father really was. It would be like listening to a CD of heavy metal and then suddenly switching to a melodic worship songs. When Jesus began to preach in Judea, His was a new voice that the people were not used to. He was hopeful, assuring, and affirming, and His words had a quality of truth about them that liberated people.

MY WORDS ARE LIFE

It is important that we know about *zoe,* so we can properly discern the voice of God. For the rest of our Christian lives we are going to have to discern God's voice, whether it comes through leadership, through well-meaning people, through prophecy, through sermons, or through Scripture. One way to tell is to see if what is said contains *zoe*.

Jesus said in John 6:63,

It is the Spirit who gives life; the flesh profits nothing. The words that I speak to you are spirit, and they are life.

The first word Jesus used for life in this verse is *zoopoieo* (GK. 2227; which means "to (re-) vitalize, make alive, give life, quicken"). The King James Version uses the word *quickeneth,* which is a revival word!

The second word for *life* in this verse is the word *zoe* (GK. 2222).

It is as if Jesus were saying, "You can tell My words by their effect. My words have a revitalizing effect, they make alive (revive), they give life and bring to life, and they quicken hearts. They are *zoe*!"

When we hear from God, it is as if something of heaven comes over us. We get some semblance of the joy of heaven. His words produce the peace of heaven. What He says causes us to experience more of the Father's heart than we had before. His words help us to know Jesus better.

We can also find *zoe* during our times of worship. Certain songs affect us; they turn our hearts toward the Lord, causing us to want more of Him.

We cannot create *zoe*. Mere words, men's words, don't affect us this way. The Beatles' music does not do this for us. It does not profit us anything, in spiritual terms anyway. What God says always leads us into a higher spiritual life.

I wish that each of my sermons was pure *zoe*, but they are not. I wish all my meetings were completely filled with *zoe*, including all the worship time, but they are not. There are usually moments of *zoe* when something of heaven enters the room and turns our hearts toward Him.

If it were really Jesus speaking, it would affect us differently. It would be something we would not soon forget. It opens more life. It leads to life and satisfies our spirits.

The devil does not have any *zoe*. He cannot make it, fake it, or even have access to it.

We must judge what has been said by the effect, not the content. Out of the abundance of His heart God's mouth speaks. He is life, so when our Father speaks, it leaves traces of His life on our hearts.

There are two basic words for the word *life* in the Bible. One of the most common words, which is translated *bios* (GK. 979) describes the material or physical life, or a natural life process. From this word, we get the word *biology*.

The other word for *life,* which is the basis of this study, is the Greek word *zoe* (GK. 2222). *Zoe* is often translated as *eternal life*, which according to the *Strong's Dictionary*, is the spiritual life. The *bios kind of life* begins at conception, but the *zoe kind of life* only begins when we are born again.

Zoe is not an eternal existence, but a quality of life which begins now and carries over into forever. Eternal life is not so much a destination or duration of life, but it is the higher spiritual life.

Experiencing more eternal life happens whenever we are going through a difficult time and we draw from the Father and the Son. We get more of His life into ours, which is *zoe*.

IF ANY MAN HEARS MY VOICE

In the Middle East, one of the most intimate things you can do with someone is to have a meal together. In Revelation 3:20, Jesus said, *"Behold, I stand at the door and knock. If anyone hears My voice and opens the door, I will come in to him and dine with him, and he with Me."*

In this, I hear Jesus saying: "Let Me in, and we'll eat together. I'm initiating this because I am hungry for your fellowship."

When Jesus speaks, it often results in our having more fellowship with Him.

Jesus is writing this to a group of Spirit-filled Christians. He revealed to John that He is often standing at the door, knocking on Christian hearts.

QUICKENED SCRIPTURE

Again, the Bible in general is the *logos*—given in general to everyone. When a part of the Bible comes alive to us, we call it "quickened" scripture. This is when a *logos* becomes a *rhema*. This is also a very common way the Lord gives us guidance and confirmation. When this happens, it becomes a life-giving word that stirs our hearts to action. The same spiritual effect cannot be imitated or contrived by our own reason. Our own ideas, no matter how biblical, do not affect us this way.

> Our own ideas, no matter how biblical, do not affect us this way.

When I was first invited to become the pastor of a small group that had been meeting in a home in Lowville, New York, Heather and I were a bit overwhelmed by the whole idea. After fasting and praying for an extended period of time, we gained assurance that it was the Lord, but we still had many obstacles in our way. There was the whole issue of being accepted by the Mennonite leadership that was responsible for the young work. I was not from a Mennonite background and would be the first to come in from the outside to stay and work within the cluster of churches in this part of the state. The other obstacle was immigration. As a Canadian citizen, I could not just go across the border and start pastoring a church. The stipulation was that I had to have been ordained for two years and have pastored for two consecutive years. I met none of the requirements. There were several other obstacles too, but those I have mentioned were huge to me. As I sought the Lord for help, I felt that He quickened to me Joshua 1:5, which says, *"No man shall stand before you."* As I read it, I heard Him say, *"No man shall stand in your way or impede your progress!"* This rhema added life to my life.

As I sat for the interviews with the Mennonite leadership, I had peace, knowing the outcome before it became clear to anyone else. I simply stood on this word, and it supported me. Then I went to the immigration office and was met with a polite but firm "No, you do not qualify to come here to work."

I found myself politely, but firmly saying, "There must be a way!" The man assured me that there was not, but I stood looking at him, praying in the spirit under my breath saying, "There must be a way." He began looking through various books and even got down and brought out some large volumes from under the counter. He looked and looked, and I prayed. Something changed, and I heard him say, more to himself than to me, "There must be a way!"

Finally, after what seemed like an hour, he came up from behind the counter with a page in his hand. He said, "I think I have found it!" As he read it aloud, he became quite excited. He was a bit disheveled and perspiring. He said, "This route is so obscure only Mormon missionaries use it. Are you a Mormon missionary by any chance?"

I said no, but it sounded like what I would be doing. He said that, if I would sign a paper promising not to work, take money, or raise offerings for my support, that he would grant me a missionary visa right then and there. I signed the paper, and he gave me my card, which was good for the next year and a half. I moved my family across the border because of the rhema of God that ushered us through all the obstacles.

ASSIGNMENT

Here are some things you can do to get your antenna up, so that your heart is receptive to what God is saying:

- Be grateful for everything.
- Be quick to respond to what you hear.
- Agree with what God is saying, rather than making excuses for the way you are.
- Avoid blaming others for your condition by taking full responsibility for the way you are.
- Be quick to repent whenever He shows you that you are doing something wrong.
- Keep track of what God has been saying to you by keeping a journal.
- Look for ways to act upon what God is saying to your own heart as you read the Scriptures.
- Treat what the Bible says the same as if He spoke it to you today. Take what He has spoken to you today the same as if it were in the Bible.

"There must be a way!"

PART EIGHT: CULTIVATING A HEARING HEART

One of the things I have spent a lot of time doing has been cultivating a hearing heart, without which it would be impossible to gain the guidance I have needed to pursue the great quest of knowing His will. Anyone who wants to learn to hear His voice will have to cultivate a hearing heart.

One time, the Lord appeared to Solomon in a dream and essentially offered the young king a blank check. "What do you want? Just ask." Imagine hearing the Lord say to you, "Ask! What shall I give you?" What would you ask for?

Here was Solomon's memorable response:

You have shown great mercy to Your servant David my father, because he walked before You in truth, in righteousness, and in uprightness of heart with You; You have continued this great kindness for him, and You have given him a son to sit on his throne, as it is this day. Now, O Lord my God, You have made Your servant king instead of my father David, but I am a little child; I do not know how to go out or come in. And Your servant is in the midst of Your people whom You have chosen, a great people, too numerous to be numbered or counted. Therefore give to Your servant an understanding heart to judge Your people, that I may discern between good and evil. For who is able to judge this great people of Yours?

This response so pleased the Lord, that God said to him:

Because you have asked this thing, and have not asked long life for yourself, nor have asked riches for yourself, nor have asked the life of your enemies, but have asked for yourself understanding to discern justice, behold, I have done according to your words; see, I have given you a wise and understanding heart, so that there has not been anyone like you before you, nor shall any like you arise after you. And I have also given you what you have not asked: both riches and honor, so that there shall not be anyone like you among the kings all your days. So if you walk in My ways, to keep My statutes and My commandments, as your father David walked, then I will lengthen your days. (1 Kings 3:4-14)

In verse 9, Solomon asked for *an understanding heart*. This can also be translated as *a hearing heart*. In this study, I wrote about how to cultivate a sensitivity to your own spirit, listening to the voice of your conscience, and following the inner witness. All of these things have enriched my life as I've applied them. They have helped me come into His purposes time and again, and because of that I wanted to share them with you. After all, if you have a hearing heart, you will be able to perceive His will, act upon it, and come into what He has for you—and this is the great key into the great quest.

> Imagine hearing the Lord say to you, "Ask! What shall I give you?"

As you think about how guidance happens within us—in the form of desires, promptings, inner "knowings," and discernment—all of this comes from having a hearing heart. I have learned to take steps or make plans, with an open, sensitive spirit, so that the Lord can direct or correct me with the slightest nudge.

I want to talk about the kind of guidance that comes from within, when our hearts lead us into doing things we would otherwise not do. Paul talked about our new nature being our guide:

> *If your spiritual nature is your guide, you are not subject to Moses' laws.* (Galatians 5:18 GWT)

CORRECTIVE GUIDANCE

I have come to trust the Lord for corrective guidance. By this I mean, I rest in the fact that He will tell me whenever I am wrong. He will do this whenever I say the wrong thing or even have wrong motives. His Spirit prompts my spirit, using my conscience to convict me. In the same way, I trust Him to show me when I am making a bad decision or going in the wrong direction. Here is how this is expressed in Scripture:

> *"Your ears shall hear a word behind you, saying, 'This is the way, walk in it,' whenever you turn to the right hand or whenever you turn to the left."* (Isaiah 30:21)

Notice this verse is saying that God speaks in our ear when we turn to the right or left. I think of this as corrective direction as I go, not something that happens before I move.

INNER ASSURANCE

Our hearts will tell us when we are praying the wrong way or longing for the wrong thing. When this happens, we will lack confidence or assurance in what we are asking for:

> *My little children, let us not love in word or in tongue, but in deed and in truth. And by this we know that we are of the truth, and shall assure our hearts before Him. For if our heart condemns us, God is greater than our heart, and knows all things. Beloved, if our heart does not condemn us, we have confidence toward God. And whatever we ask we receive from Him, because we keep His commandments and do those things that are pleasing in His sight. And this is His commandment: that we should believe on the name of His Son Jesus Christ and love one another, as He gave us commandment.* (1 John 3:18-23)

If it is not God's will, we will not have the *confidence* to boldly ask for it:

Now this is the confidence that we have in Him, that if we ask anything according to His will, He hears us. And if we know that He hears us, whatever we ask, we know that we have the petitions that we have asked of Him. (1 John 5:14-15)

Our confidence and assurance stem from the same source. You can see the part this assurance plays, in terms of getting direction, in the story of Paul trying to find where he was to go next:

*Now when they had gone throughout Phrygia and the region of Galatia, and were forbidden of the Holy Ghost to preach the word in Asia, after they were come to Mysia, they assayed to go into Bithynia: but the Spirit suffered them not. And they passing by Mysia came down to Troas. And a vision appeared to Paul in the night; there stood a man of Macedonia, and prayed him, saying, Come over into Macedonia, and help us. And after he had seen the vision, immediately we endeavoured to go into Macedonia, **assuredly gathering** that the Lord had called us for to preach the gospel unto them.* (Acts 16:6-10 KJV)

This assurance that they felt acted like a compass, leading the way for them.

TRUE NORTH—GUIDED BY OUR CONSCIENCE

No matter where you stand on earth, whenever you hold a compass in your hand, it will always point north. It is not the compass itself, but something that God put in the earth. It is perfectly accurate under all conditions, whether it is sunny, overcast, night-time, or day-time, something our high-tech navigational devices cannot always do. The simple compass has given us an easy and inexpensive way to keep ourselves oriented.

In the same way, our conscience was designed to help orient us spiritually, letting us know what is right from wrong in all things. I believe that the conscience is actually the voice of our spirit, which came from God originally, having been breathed into the nostrils of Adam, making us like God. This is true of all people, everywhere, whether they are believers or not:

For when the Gentiles, which have not the law, do by nature the things contained in the law, these, having not the law, are a law unto themselves: Which show the work of the law written in their hearts, their conscience also bearing witness, and their thoughts the mean while accusing or else excusing one another; in the day when God shall judge the secrets of men by Jesus Christ according to my gospel. (Romans 2:14-16)

If we could learn to respond to our spirit, cultivating a sensitivity to it, it would help us know right from wrong, not just morally, but whenever we need guidance or spiritual direction as well. Notice that it *bears witness*. This means it works within us in a confirming way, giving us a sense that what we are doing

> I believe that the conscience is actually the voice of our spirit.

is right. Paul said that it can also *accuse* or *excuse* us, which is what we call "a check" or "a release" in our spirit. Sometimes these two affects are described as having a red light or green light within us. Our spirit bears witness, helping us to have a sense of knowing, beyond our ability to know with our understanding, which is an invaluable part of guidance. The most amazing part of it to me, is how accurate it is, like a compass finding true north every time.

PAUL CALLED HIS CONSCIENCE AS A WITNESS

Paul often called his conscience as a witness whenever he was falsely accused of wrongdoing:

> *Then Paul, looking earnestly at the council, said, "Men and brethren, I have lived in all good conscience before God until this day."* (Acts 23:1)

> *"This being so, I myself always strive to have a conscience without offense toward God and men."* (24:16)

> *The Spirit Himself **bears witness with our spirit** that we are children of God, and if children, then heirs; heirs of God and joint heirs with Christ, if indeed we suffer with Him, that we may also be glorified together.* (Romans 8:16-17)

> *I tell the truth in Christ, I am not lying, my conscience also bearing me witness in the Holy Spirit, that I have great sorrow and continual grief in my heart.* (9:1-2)

Here are some other verses that refer to the testimony of the conscience:

> *For our boasting is this:* **the testimony of our conscience** *that we conducted ourselves in the world in simplicity and godly sincerity, not with fleshly wisdom but by the grace of God, and more abundantly toward you.* (2 Corinthians 1:12)

However, it is possible to ruin our consciences so that they do not work properly. This is done by living a life of lying and hypocrisy, which is a violation of our integrity:

> *Speaking lies in hypocrisy, having their own conscience seared with a hot iron.* (1 Timothy 4:2)

The word *seared* conveys the idea of something being desensitized or cauterized at the nerve endings.

In Proverbs 6:28, it describes becoming immoral to the point that we are like a man walking on hot coals and his feet become seared.

Some believers ignore the warnings of their conscience, choosing to be ruled by feelings or leaning on their own understanding instead until they become shipwrecked in their faith:

Having faith and a good conscience, which some having rejected, concerning the faith have suffered shipwreck. (1 Timothy 1:19)

THE INTEGRITY OF OUR HEART

Basically, having integrity involves being honest with ourselves. It is being honest with what our consciences have been saying. This is a major ingredient in guidance. There are a number of key verses that show how humanity has relied upon this integrity to help guide us:

Let integrity and uprightness preserve me, for I wait for You. (Psalm 25:21)

He who walks with integrity walks securely. (Proverbs 10:9)

The integrity of the upright will guide them. (11:3)

Integrity involves being honest with ourselves and others, sifting our motives before the Lord, letting Him search our hearts. He can help us see if our motives are self-pleasing, people-pleasing, or God-pleasing. No matter which form of guidance we use, it all hinges on the integrity of our hearts.

The goal is not to be infallible people, but to become people of integrity.

When we go through conflicts with people, we need to sort through all the accusations thrown at us, examining them for any truth, sorting out whatever it is that actually divides us. These times often test the depth and development of our integrity.

UMPIRE OF THE HEART

There is a peace which God uses to help guide us, especially in our relationships with others. It is a peace that we cannot rationally produce within ourselves. Paul described it as being like an inner "umpire" of the heart, when he said, *"Let the peace of God rule in your hearts"* (Colossians 3:15).

The word rule here, in *The Strong's Concordance*, literally means "letting the peace of God act as an umpire in our hearts."

An umpire in sports helps us to know objectively whether we are in or out, right or wrong.

THE INNER KNOWING—THE ANOINTING WITHIN

Besides having a good conscience and integrity, we have another tool within us called *the anointing within*. This comes when Jesus first enters our hearts. Because He is the Anointed One, He smears our hearts with Himself. The effect of this is that it helps our hearts know what is biblically true and what is not, long before our theology has had a chance to develop:

Because He is the Anointed One, He smears our hearts with Himself.

But you have an anointing from the Holy One, and you know all things. (1 John 2:20)

But the anointing which you have received from Him abides in you, and you do not need that anyone teach you; but as the same anointing teaches you concerning all things, and is true, and is not a lie, and just as it has taught you, you will abide in Him. (v. 27)

We can know at a heart level if what we are being taught is right or wrong. This is a special protection the Lord has installed in us to keep us safe from deception. But in order for it to work, we need to follow the anointing at work within our hearts rather than our heads.

As a new believer, I had a number of occasions to see this work on my behalf. My head would say that certain teachings must be all right because they were being taught in a church or at well-respected conference, but my heart said it was wrong. This can be ignored or overridden, but it is never wrong.

The spirit of man is the candle of the Lord, searching all the inward parts of the belly. (Proverbs 20:27 KJV)

Notice that it is the spirit of man that the Lord uses to search us. God always uses it in the guidance process. In the New Testament, we are told that it is our spirits that know us:

For what man knows the things of a man except the spirit of the man which is in him? Even so no one knows the things of God except the Spirit of God. (1 Corinthians 2:11 KJV)

Just as God's Spirit knows His heart, His thinking, His motives, His desires, and His way of doing things, our spirits know what is going on inside of us. God uses our spirits in every form of guidance.

THINGS WE CAN DO NOW

- **Cultivate a sensitive spirit.** This comes from being quick to repent, learning to be quiet, meditating upon His Word, and walking in worship.

- **Come before Him in worship.** I find that beginning by worshipping Him, both in my natural language and with my heavenly, not only opens my spirit to His Spirit, but let's Him know that I want more than mere solutions to my problems.

- **Learn to unplug.** He will not compete with your cell phone, music, or constant talking.

- **Learn to take a sabbath** on a regular basis, where you learn to be quiet and still.

- **Learn to "come aside"** in the wilderness (see my study notes on this).

- **Sort out on paper** what you really want to ask Him about.

- **Miss some meals.** You may have to get in the habit of fasting on a weekly basis. If there is a fast track, this is it.

- **Pray in tongues.** Paul prayed in tongues often. It is one way to get past the limits of our own understanding:

  For if I pray in a tongue, my spirit prays, but my understanding is unfruitful. What is the conclusion then? I will pray with the spirit, and I will also pray with the understanding. I will sing with the spirit, and I will also sing with the understanding. (1 Corinthians 14:14-15)

ASSIGNMENT

Take the time to look up other verses in the Bible about the conscience:

But we have renounced the hidden things of shame, not walking in craftiness nor handling the word of God deceitfully, but by manifestation of the truth commending ourselves to every man's conscience in the sight of God. (2 Corinthians 4:2)

I thank God, whom I serve with a pure conscience, as my forefathers did, as without ceasing I remember you in my prayers night and day. (2 Timothy 1:3)

PART NINE: GUIDELINES TO GUIDANCE

I have spent a lifetime trying to find guidance for God's immediate will in my daily life. It has been a great adventure and has brought a lot of pleasure to my spirit and resulted in praise to God. However, there are those today who teach that there really is no specific will of God to be sought and that we should just do whatever comes to mind in the moment. This has become a popular thing to teach, for a number of reasons, but how does this line up with Jesus' view of the will of God, specifically in relationship to His disciples?

Jesus often told His disciples about God's will, teaching them how to pray that it be done on earth as it was in heaven (see Matthew 6:10). He also demonstrated in front of them what being surrendered to the Father's will looks like, rather than doing what He felt to do or would naturally do. Suffering and dying on the cross (see Luke 22:42) is an example of this.

The disciples also witnessed a vision where Moses and Elijah came to Jesus to discuss what manner of death He would die (see Luke 9:30-31).

Later, Jesus told Peter what manner of death he would eventually experience (John 21:18-19). Both of these are a glimpse or revelation of God's will.

Jesus gave His disciples specific direction:

- He told them to go to the other side of the lake while He stayed on shore (Matthew 14:22; Mark 6:45).

- He told them which side of the boat to cast their nets, to which they responded, *"Nevertheless, at thy word [rhema]"* (Luke 5:5; John 21:6).

- He gave them directions—to finding a donkey to ride on—and He also told them how to find an upper room for the Last Supper (Matthew 21:1-3; Luke 19:29-31; 22:9-11).

- When the problem of paying taxes came up, He told Peter how to find a miraculous provision for them (Matthew 17:24-27).

- He sent them out, doing evangelism, with specific directions (Mark 6:7-9; Luke 10:1).

- He seemed to be aware of being in God's timetable, telling Herod that He would not meet with him because He had an itinerary laid out (Luke 13:31-33).

- Once He knew the timetable and specific direction, He set His face as a flint to do it (Luke 9:51-56).

He also answered all of the people's questions, both theological and directional.

Jesus not only led His disciples, but He gave them direction and personal guidance. What He did for them, He will do for us today.

GUIDANCE IN THE BOOK OF ACTS

There are those today telling us to do something, whatever comes naturally to mind, totally discounting the sovereign or supernatural aspect of guidance from the Lord. Rather than arguing about this, let's go to the book of Acts to see what the apostles experienced concerning divine guidance:

- The apostles sought the Lord's will by casting lots to see who should replace Judas (Acts 1:24-26).
- Angels were used to free the apostles from prison and to give them specific direction (5:19-20; 12:7-8).
- The living Christ spoke to Saul on the road to Damascus, telling him where to go next (9:4-6).
- The disciple Ananias was given a vision to go to where Saul was staying, giving him a specific address and telling him to pray for him to receive healing (9:10-16).
- Cornelius was instructed by an angel in a vision to send for Peter and was given a specific address (9:10-16; 10:3-6).
- Peter was given direction from God through a vision, and a word of knowledge, and by the Holy Spirit speaking within (10:19-20).
- Philip was given specific direction both by an angel and by the Spirit speaking, which led to the conversion of the Ethiopian eunuch (8:26, 29).
- The prophet Agabus prophetically foretold everyone that a famine was coming (11:27-30).
- The Holy Spirit spoke concerning releasing Barnabas and Saul into their apostolic ministries. This was confirmed by the leadership of the church at Antioch (13:2).
- Paul and his team were forbidden by the Holy Spirit to go into Asia Minor (16:6-7). It turned out to be just a matter of timing, and he eventually went there to start some great churches.
- Paul was directed to go Macedonia in a night vision (16:9-10).
- Paul was told to remain in Corinth to preach (18:9-10).
- Paul was forewarned about what awaited him in Jerusalem (20:23; 21:4, 11).
- Jesus appeared to Paul, telling him to flee Jerusalem (22:18, 21).

- Paul was told that he would live to be God's witness at Rome (23:11).

- Paul perceived by an inner witness that the ship he was on was in peril (Acts 27:10).

- Paul was told by an angel that he would be saved in a shipwreck (27:22-26).

When we take the spiritual or supernatural out of guidance, it leaves a big hole. Some authors are doing this, I think, for two reasons. First, they are reacting to young people whom they have met who are so desirous to know God's will that they have become anxious or unstable. These authors feel the need to debunk the idea of our needing to seek God to show us His immediate will.

It is true that people often become over-anxious about God's will, which is counterproductive. Nobody hears very well when they are afraid or anxious. It causes their antenna to go down, but we should not throw out the concept of seeking God because of this.

Secondly, we all have met those who over-spiritualize guidance, making it so super-spiritual that it negates the use of any common sense. While this does happen, and all this "God told me" can be a bit off-putting, especially when it turns out that God was not speaking, we should not dismiss all spiritual guidance.

In the back of this book, in Addendum Three, I have included a list of promises and principles of guidance.

SUBJECTIVE AND OBJECTIVE GUIDANCE

Guidance usually begins in our hearts, which is called *subjective guidance*. This includes hearing the voice of the Lord, having an inner peace, or an inspired idea. Our guidance should not be based solely on subjective guidance because:

There is a way that seems right to a man but the end thereof is destruction. (Proverbs 14:12)

We also need objective guidance, which is guidance that comes from outside of ourselves. This type of guidance is not dependent upon what we think or how we feel. Objective guidance includes doing what is in Scripture, receiving wise counsel, hearing prophecy, and being in agreement with others.

Here is a verse that illustrates the difference between subjective and objective guidance:

The preparations of the heart belong to man, but the answer of the tongue is from the Lord. All the ways of a man are pure in his own eyes, but the Lord weighs the spirits. Commit your works to the Lord, and your thoughts will be established. (Proverbs 16:1-3)

The plans and preparations of our heart are subjective because they occur within us. To us, it's what we think seems right, but the Lord will weigh our motives. Then, as we commit our works to Him, letting Him have the final say, He will establish His plans objectively.

God tends to speak to us in part, like pieces of a puzzle that need to come together to get the full picture. Perhaps this is why the apostle Paul said,

For we know in part, and we prophesy in part. (1 Corinthians 13:9)

Some pieces of this puzzle are subjective while others are objective.

Big needs require big guidance. Everyday circumstances require little guidance. We should not make a major decision based on subjective guidance alone. My rule of thumb is that I need His confirmation on any decision that presumes upon the future.

For example, we should not buy a house because we have a peace about it. Likewise, we don't fast and pray all day to decide whether or not we should buy beans or peas. We need a balance of both subjective and objective guidance. If we have only one or the other, it is like trying to fly with one wing.

SUBJECTIVE GUIDANCE

Here are some examples of subjective guidance:

1. **Guidance through peace:** There is a peace which God uses to help guide us, and we cannot rationally produce it ourselves. God can give us a peace that surpasses understanding. This peace was described by Paul as an inner umpire of the heart in Colossians 3:15. When he said, let the peace of God "rule in your hearts."

   The Strong's Concordance defines this phrase as "letting the peace of God umpire." An umpire helps us to judge whether we are in or out, right or wrong.

2. **Guidance through integrity:** No matter which method of guidance is used, it all hinges on the integrity of our hearts.

   The integrity of the upright will guide them, but the perversity of the unfaithful will destroy them. (Proverbs 11:3)

   Sift your motives honestly before the Lord. Lay your motives bare before His searchlight and look for the self-pleasing, people-pleasing, and God-pleasing kinds of motives that lay beneath the surface of your thinking. I learned that, if I am reluctant to talk my intentions over with the Lord, then I am set on doing my own thing.

3. **Guidance through wisdom:** When it comes to getting guidance, we will need a lot of wisdom. One facet of wisdom is seeing your life and circumstances through His eyes. Perspective is everything!

   If any of you lacks wisdom, let him ask of God, who gives to all liberally and without reproach, and it will be given to him. But let him ask in faith, with no doubting, for he who doubts is like a wave of the sea driven and tossed by the wind. For let not that man suppose that he will receive anything from the Lord; he is a double-minded man, unstable in all his ways. (James 1:5-8)

4. **Guidance through prudence**: Ask yourself, "Does this guidance make sense?" Prudence is a cousin to wisdom. It basically means "to be discerning" but is often rendered "good judgment" in some Bible translations. I often mentally change the word to "common sense." Remember, the book of Proverbs was written in order to:

   Give prudence to the simple, to the young man knowledge and discretion; a wise man will hear and increase learning, and a man of understanding will attain wise counsel. (Proverbs 1:1-5)

   I have found that all of the guidance God has given me over the years has been both sane and practical. Guidance should make sense, even though it will always require faith to grasp it. We have to find the balance between being fool-hardy, super-spiritual, and relying on the limits of our own understanding (see Proverbs 3:5). Remember, our lives have been planned by Someone who thinks like an architect. We should be able to look back and see that our way has been progressive, with one thing being connected to another. It should also look orderly and even beautiful.

5. **Guidance through inner assurance:** As we move along in a certain direction, following His leading, we gain more assurance as we go. We gain confidence as we walk toward His will. The apostle Paul was led this way in Acts 16:10:

   Now after he had seen the vision, immediately we sought to go to Macedonia, gathering assurance that the Lord had called us to preach the gospel to them.

6. **Guidance through inner witness:** It is essential that we learn to rely on the inner witness of His Spirit, which affects our spirits.

   And it is the Spirit who bears witness, because the Spirit is truth. (1 John 5:6)

   He who believes in the Son of God has the witness in himself. (v. 10)

   His Spirit bears witness within our spirits, not just about being born again, but about the rightness or wrongness of whatever we do. These "checks and releases" are essential to finding God's will. The Bible uses language such as "The Spirit bade me go," or "The Spirit forbade me." I refer to this as a red light or green light in our hearts. Examples of this can be found in the following verses:

The red light:

Now when they had gone through Phrygia and the region of Galatia, they were forbidden by the Holy Spirit to preach the word in Asia. After they had come to Mysia, they tried to go into Bithynia, but the Holy Spirit would not permit them. (Acts 16:6-7)

The green light:

And a vision appeared to Paul in the night. A man of Macedonia stood and pleaded with him, saying, "Come over to Macedonia and help us." Now after he had seen the vision immediately we sought to go to Macedonia, concluding that the Lord had called us to preach the gospel to them. (Acts 16:9-10)

Other forms of subjective guidance include visions and dreams, hearing the voice of the Lord, or simply feeling led. While guidance usually starts at a subjective level, it should be established objectively.

OBJECTIVE GUIDANCE

Objective forms of guidance, which God often uses to confirm what is happening inside of us are not based on what we think or how we feel. This form of guidance is based on a reliable outside source.

1. **Guidance through Scripture**: Does your guidance follow a biblical pattern or precedent? God never gives personal guidance that contradicts what is written in the Bible. You should always ask, "Where can I find this in the Bible?"

2. **Guidance through authority**: Beware any time you intentionally conceal your plans or refuse to submit your direction to those in authority. This usually indicates that we want our will more than God's. God speaks mainly through the authority structure He created.

   Each area of authority should speak within their own respective area of authority. Areas of authority include: your parents, your spouse, your pastor or overseer, your employer, and your government. For example, you don't ask your boss to speak to church issues, or the government about how to raise your children.

3. **Guidance through a multitude of counselors**: Learn to rest in the wisdom of a multitude of counselors. A multitude does not mean every-

body and their uncle. Choose two or three people who have earned the right to speak into your life and those who have a desire to be led by the Lord in all their ways. Choose those whose own lives have been shaped by gaining guidance from God.

Where there is no counsel, the people fall; but in the multitude of counselors there is safety. (Proverbs 11:14)

Without counsel, plans go awry, but in the multitude of counselors they are established. (15:22)

For by wise counsel you will wage your own war, and in a multitude of counselors there is safety. (24:6)

4. **Guidance through agreement**: The Bible asks, *"Can two walk together except they are agreed?"* (Amos 3:3). To me, being in agreement with my spouse is actually a higher form of guidance than a prophetic word.

    We should always be in agreement with those who are going to be affected the most by our guidance. They should also be included in the process of discerning the will of the Lord, if they are expected to accept our leadership. For example, if a husband desires to move, the spouse needs to be able to be part of that decision. A wise leader will try to bring everyone along in the process so we can peaceably enjoy the direction of the Lord.

5. **Guidance through seeing the need**: Seeing the need can sometimes be all the guidance we need to know His will. When the disciples saw the people's need, they told Jesus about it. He, in turn, made them responsible to meet it:

    When the day began to wear away, the twelve came and said to Him, "Send the multitude away, that they may go into the surrounding towns and country, and lodge and get provisions; for we are in a deserted place here." But He said to them, "You give them something to eat." (Luke 9:12-13)

    Today when we see people in need and tell Jesus about them, we call it intercession, but if we had ears to hear, we would hear Him say the same thing to us. "You do something about it. What do you have? You must give it to them, and trust that I will bless it."

    After the disciples saw the need, they became responsible to do something about it. They also needed His ability to bless their efforts: *"Then He took the five loaves and the two fish, and looking up to heaven, He blessed and broke them, and gave them to the disciples to set before the multitude."* (Luke 9:16)

At the same time, not every need is a call to do something. It takes time and maturity to sort out what is and what is not a need, so that we are not driven by guilt.

6. **Guidance through provision**: God's provision is a powerful form of objective guidance. The reason this can be a good form of confirmation is because we can seldom control the flow of finances. (If we could have more, we all would have more.) If you are following what you think is the leading of the Lord, but the money does not come in, you should really step back and consider your course. The old adage is true, "Where God guides, He provides."

LED BY COUNSEL

Much of what I know now about discerning God's will has come out of my own experiences, both positive and negative. I cannot tell you which has taught me more about guidance, my successes or my failures. There have been plenty of both. I have missed it many times when making small decisions, purchases, and travel plans. I wish I had every dollar back that I have misspent on computer-related purchases. Don't you?

I have missed it many times in my judgments of people, both on their ability and maturity, but I can honestly say that the leadership team I led never had to stand before the congregation and say that we missed it in terms of our guidance or decisions during all these years of pastoral ministry. This is due in large part because when it comes to making decisions on behalf of others, I always seek counsel and allow the necessary time it takes for God to establish my ways with the help of others.

There are two significant problems I see in charismatic circles these days. First, there are pastors who lead their churches prophetically. In other words, they have a word from God or a vision for everything. They go off in various directions because someone prophesied it. This has led to many hurts and divisions and has misrepresented how local church authority works.

As church leaders, we make hundreds of decisions on behalf of the congregation every year, but we should ask our leadership team members to give us their honest counsel, rather than the word of the Lord. We do not encourage language like, "The Lord told me," "I feel led," or "God gave me this idea." This causes others to be reluctant to share their own opinions. They may not be comfortable contradicting what someone else says is God's leading. If they choose to use this language, then we judge it as prophecy.

We can safely arrive at God's will together by open and honest sharing. Picture a funnel in the middle of the table. Everyone puts in his or her opinion, counsel, and concerns, and what comes out in the end will likely be what the

> *I cannot tell you which has taught me more about guidance, my successes or my failures.*

Lord is saying to us as leaders. We need to trust that God will give us sound judgment, if only because of our responsibility to serve the members and make decisions on their behalf. I do not remember the last time we had to reverse a decision or undo a major problem caused by the guidance our board has found for our congregation.

GODLY GOD-GIVEN AUTHORITY

This section can sound self-serving, because I am someone in a position of authority, but I have always been a man under authority, and this has proven to be a real benefit in my own life through the years. I believe that those in authority in our lives can "see things" in us that we cannot see.

It is easier to submit to those godly pastors who *"watch for our souls."*

Obey those who rule over you, and be submissive, for they watch out for your souls, as those who must give account. Let them do so with joy and not with grief, for that would be unprofitable for you. (Hebrews 13:17)

Also, people in authority can easily get "the word of the Lord" by virtue of their position, not their perfection or personality or because of their great spirituality. Here is a story that illustrates this in the life of Jesus, concerning His own high priest:

Then the chief priests and the Pharisees gathered a council and said, "What shall we do? For this Man works many signs. If we let Him alone like this, everyone will believe in Him, and the Romans will come and take away both our place and nation." And one of them, Caiaphas, being high priest that year, said to them, "You know nothing at all, nor do you consider that it is expedient for us that one man should die for the people, and not that the whole nation should perish. Now this he did not say on his own authority; but being high priest that year he prophesied that Jesus would die for the nation, and not for that nation only, but also that He would gather together in one the children of God who were scattered abroad. Then, from that day on, they plotted to put Him to death." (John 11:47-53)

> When we avoid submitting our guidance to others, it usually indicates that we want our own will more than we want God's will.

We should submit our guidance to those in authority, humbly asking for their counsel, all the while, asking God to confirm it. We should beware any time we allow a prophetic word or our own personal guidance to put a wedge between ourselves and godly authority. If we deliberately avoid submitting our guidance to them, then we need a heart adjustment. I believe that a breakdown in our relationship with godly authority is the number one way the enemy brings people into deception. When we avoid submitting our guidance to others, it usually indicates that we want our own will more than we want God's will.

GOD ESTABLISHES HIS WILL

God wants to establish or confirm His will. The effect of having it established can be profound. Imagine walking tentatively in a muddy swamp, not being sure of what you will step on next, or if you will sink to the hip in mud. Suddenly, you begin to feel something hard and solid beneath your feet. As you feel around with your toes, you realize that there is a concrete sidewalk under your feet, heading in the direction you are going. Not only can you now walk with confidence, but you can run. This is what it's like when God's will is established in your life.

Here are two powerful promises you can stand on, where God promises to establish your way:

Ponder the path of your feet and let all your ways be established. (Proverbs 4:26)

Commit your works to the Lord, and your plans will be established. (16:3)

If you look for the word *confirmation* the way I am using it here, you will not find it. However, *confirmation* can be found in the Greek word for *edification*, which is *oikodomē* (GK. 3619). This is an architectural term that means to confirm or build up. If you do a word study of the word *edify* or *edification* in the New Testament, you will find Bible references to support the way I am using it. A clear example of this is found in 1 Corinthians 14:3, where it says:

But he who prophesies speaks edification and exhortation and comfort to men.

Prophecy is a practical and powerful way that God often uses to confirm what He is doing. This explains why there were several prophets speaking to Israel at one time.

Whenever a word is spoken, there is usually a gulf between where we are spiritually and where we end up when it finally comes to pass. Remember, God calls things that are not as though they already were (see Romans 4:17). It's very likely that we will go through a lot of growing before the promises come to pass.

> Remember, God calls things that are not as though they already were.

BUILDING IN SAFEGUARDS

This issue of getting spiritual direction or guidance is difficult to navigate and not without some risk. It can be made a little easier by embracing the following safeguards:

- **We must never elevate anything above God's written Word.** It is always greater than prophecy, greater than our own understanding, and greater than the commandments of man.

- **We must be in agreement with those who will be affected by the guidance being given.** Having godly agreement between a husband and wife is a greater form of guidance than prophecy by itself.

- **We must never accept any prophecy that puts a wedge between us and the godly authorities that have been put in place to watch over our souls.**

- **We must never devalue the need for practical wisdom, common sense, or the counsel of others.** The Scripture says that there is safety in the multitude of counselors, not the multitude of prophecies.

- **God will always establish what He is really saying.** If it isn't established, it wasn't Him speaking.

SUMMARY: A VISION THAT HOLDS

What holds your interest today? What are you shooting for? Here is a short list of the things that the apostle Paul had for his personal goals, goals that still fired his zeal after all he had been through. This study is based upon what he wrote in Philippians 3:2-16. He wrote this epistle from Rome during what we now know was to be the last two years of his life. At this stage of his life, he had been everywhere and done everything. He had been on the front row of what God was doing in the earth, but his past accomplishments could no longer hold his interest.

> *He had been on the front row of what God was doing in the earth.*

He sounds like many pastors who, after twenty-five or thirty years in the ministry, don't have much to shoot for anymore. They have spent all their "firsts," and after a while, it is hard to get excited about more numbers, more trips, and more meetings.

> *But what things were gain to me, these I have counted loss for Christ. Yet indeed I also that I may gain Christ and be found in Him, not having my own righteousness, which is from the law, but that which is through faith in Christ, the righteousness which is from God by faith; that I may know Him and the power of His resurrection, and the fellowship of His sufferings, being conformed to His death, if, by any means, I may attain to the resurrection from the dead.*

Amazing! His goal was still to win Christ or to have His approval. He wanted to experience being right with God, not by doing everything right, but by being right with Him by faith alone. He wanted to know Jesus' resurrection power. There is an unusual quality about real miraculous power. You can never see enough of it. Paul also wanted to experience more of the fellowship of Christ's suffering. There is a special place of fellowship, beyond words, whenever you go through something He Himself went through— persecution, slander, rejection, abandonment. Jesus comes to you. No words are really necessary; there is a sweet knowing that you have tasted something He has tasted. It is the highest level of communion with Christ. It is so rich that Paul embraced whatever happened to him just so he could taste it again. It kept him going through the beatings, the travel, the trials, the time adrift on the open sea, the time spent in prison just because he knew Jesus would be at every trial and visit him in every cell.

Then Paul does something that every pastor should find solace in. In verses 12 to 14, he says, "I have not arrived yet, I have attained all there is to attain, but I press on." That's a man with vision talking. This is a vision that holds. He said he still wanted to experience more of the purposes God had for him in Christ. Then he gives this nugget of advice, which is permission for the rest of us, enabling us to do the same:

> *But one thing I do, forgetting those things which are behind and reaching forward to those things which are ahead, I press toward the goal for the prize of the upward call of God in Christ Jesus.*

He wrote in verses 15 and 16,

> *Therefore let us, as many as are mature, have this mind; and if in anything you think otherwise, God will reveal even this to you. Nevertheless, to the degree that we have already attained, let us walk by the same rule, let us be of the same mind.*

This is advice from someone who is mature to those who are maturing. In fact, this is how you measure real maturity. If you don't do this, and you continue to rest on your laurels and draw your sense of success from the past, from statistics you have achieved, or places you have been, then God will expose this for what it is. These things do not matter much. They are dung. They will not hold your interest for long. They will not satisfy you until the end. You still have to shoot for something more. There are valuable lessons you have learned over time. Don't forget them, but forget all the rest, and press in for more. Be current with God.

Kellogg's Corn Flakes had an interesting slogan for an advertising campaign they created to get people to come back to the cereal of their childhood by invoking a memory of eating Corn Flakes as a kid. "Taste them again, for the first time."

There are a lot of things we need to taste again as if it were the first time. What was it like when you first met Jesus? For me, I just wanted to be with Him all the time, so I talked to Him constantly. I never really thought of it as prayer at all. I would tell Him my concerns, ask Him questions, tell Him my wonderings, and often sang to Him. That was my first love experience. I couldn't get enough of reading about Jesus in the Bible.

But like a marriage, over time, all the original romance fades with the realities of life and the busyness of work and responsibilities, but a wise couple will

> "Taste them again, for the first time."

always try to recapture that first love over and over again, in order to keep their marriage fresh.

To do this, I have set as one of my goals a determination to get alone with the Lord and just be. I tell Him that I am not coming to Him as a pastor, but simply as a friend. Rather than asking for anything, I just spend time expressing my love and appreciation for Him. In doing this, I am tasting and seeing that Lord is good. I am tasting Him again for the first time.

PART TEN: QUESTIONS AND ANSWERS

Q. What about all the evil in the world, like disease, crime, and accidents? I cannot believe that God would allow these things to exist, much less allow them to happen to the innocent. If He is sovereign, doesn't that mean He both created and allows these things to happen?

A. Take the weather for example. God promised rain and good weather to good people and bad weather for bad people, like a blessing and a curse (see Leviticus 26:4), but in the end, when the curse came, even good people are peripherally affected by it (see Matthew 5:45).

There are accounts in the Bible of God altering the weather for His purposes, as in the case of droughts and famines, hailstorms, and floods. We can also see where the devil used the weather for his purposes, like in the story of Job, where a tornado caused a house to fall on people (see Job 1:13-22). Satan is called "the god of this world" because he has some authority down here (see 2 Corinthians 4:4). Then there are life-threatening storms like the ones we read about on the Sea of Galilee which Jesus spoke to, and they calmed down. Jesus did not mention what the source of the storm was, whether it was of God or the devil, because it seemed to be beside the point. He simply used it for His glory and the disciples' good.

The same could be said about sickness. In the Bible, God promised health for those who followed Him and sickness for those who didn't, like a blessing and a curse. There are accounts in the Bible of God using sickness and healing for His purposes, and we can also see where there were times when the devil used it for his purposes (John 10:10).

Then there were ailments that people brought upon themselves, through their sin and disobedience. When Jesus healed the man who had been blind from birth, the disciples had two root causes in mind, which to them explained why this happened to him; either he sinned or his parents sinned. But Jesus said it was neither of these, but for the glory of God (John 9:2-3).

Part of the problem with all of these things, including wars and social disasters, is that we like to categorically attribute them to a single source, but as we can see, it is much more complex than this. For me, I keep my child-like simplicity and the peace that comes with it.

Somehow David did this. Even though he was a mighty warrior, the greatest king, and one of the richest men on earth, he became like a child in his approach to life:

Lord, my heart is not haughty, nor mine eyes lofty: neither do I exercise myself in great matters, or in things too high for me. Surely I have behaved and quieted myself, as a child that is weaned of his mother: my soul is even as a weaned child. Let Israel hope in the Lord from henceforth and forever. (Psalm 131)

I simply rest in the idea that there will be a Day, a Judgment Day, when everything will be reveled for what it was, including what the devil and his angels did, what God and His angels did, and what the will of man accomplished in the earth. The sum total of that judgement will be that God is just and does all things rightly. We will bow down and worship Him for His work in the earth and His profound mercy. Then, *"God will wipe away every tear from our eyes; there shall be no more death, nor sorrow, nor crying. There shall be no more pain, for the former things have passed away"* (Revelation 21:4). I look to this Day, rather than trying to make judgments about all that happens now in this fallen world.

Q. What about Christians? They get sick too and have accidents. Why does He allow these things to happen to good people?

A. You are right, it does happen, but there is not a single answer that tells us exactly why. What I do know for certain is that He has promised that, whatever happens to us, He is able to turn it around for our good (benefit) and that He does this for those He loves and those who are aligned with His will:

And we know that all things work together for good to them that love God, to them who are the called according to his purpose. (Romans 8:28)

THE THREE WILLS OF GOD

Q. You talk about God's ultimate and immediate will, but aren't there three levels of God's will—good, acceptable, and perfect—according to Romans 12:1-3?

A. You are referring to one of the verses most often quoted from the New Testament concerning God's will:

I beseech you therefore, brethren, by the mercies of God, that you present your bodies a living sacrifice, holy, acceptable to God, which is your reasonable service. And do not be conformed to this world, but be transformed by the renewing of your mind, that you may prove what is that good and acceptable and perfect will of God. (Romans 12:1-3)

Like many of us, I had also been taught the three primary degrees to God's will, which went something like this:

1. God has a perfect will for us, which is the highest of the three. This is the will of God where everything that happens is successful. It is apparent when everything is synchronized, intersecting the right people with the right events at the right time. This is hard to find, but worth the effort.

2. God's good will is good, but not the best. It is the "OK will of God." The difficulties in life may not be His express will for us, but as long as you

learn from them, it is OK. It is like a child who benefits from a burn; at least he learns not to touch the stove again. This will is good, but not great.

3. God has an acceptable will, which is often translated as "the permissive will of God." This is where God allows something to happen to us, but it is not what He really wanted in the first place. His perfect will was missed somewhere along the way, so was His good will, so this is plan "C." Israel's forty years in the wilderness is often the example given for this. So was Israel's getting a king. Clearly, this is His lowest will, which is actually not very acceptable to any of us.

This interpretation of Romans 12:2, however, has complicated my life and the lives of others who sincerely want to follow the Lord. I understand the rationale behind this teaching; we are supposed to aspire to go for God's best and not settle for anything less, but when difficulties and conflicts arise, it allows for too much condemnation and doubt. Here is another way of interpreting this verse. Perhaps God's will is all three—good, acceptable, and perfect—and all at the same time.

GOOD

God's will is always for our benefit. This is confirmed by Romans 8:28:

And we know that all things work together for good to them that love God, to them who are the called according to his purpose.

According to the *Strong's Greek Dictionary* the word *good* is most generally rendered *beneficial*:

GOOD GK. 18 *agathos*; "good" (in and sense, often as noun):— benefit, good (-s, things), well.

ACCEPTABLE

The way we find out if something is God's will is by asking if it is acceptable to God. Would it be well-pleasing to Him? This is the actual definition of this word, as taken from the *Strong's Concordance*:

ACCEPTABLE GK. 2101. *euarestos*; from GK. 2095 and GK. 701; fully agreeable:— acceptable (-ted), well-pleasing.

In Ephesians 5:8-10, we are told to find what is acceptable to God:

For you were once darkness, but now you are light in the Lord. Walk as children of light (for the fruit of the Spirit is in all goodness, righteousness, and truth), finding out what is acceptable to the Lord.

PERFECT WILL

The word *perfect* in Scripture rarely means impeccable or infallible, as we think of perfect. Nor does it mean flawless-precision. It could be translated *complete*.

> **PERFECT** GK. 5046. *teleios*; complete (in various applications of labor, growth, mental and moral character, etc.) completeness:— of full age, man, perfect.

This means that when we live our lives according to what pleases the Lord, it is fulfilling, causing us to feel complete. So, I find more peace in the idea of God having an ultimate will and how I need to bring it into the immediate situation through my faith and submission.

HOW NARROW IS GOD'S WILL?

Q. Some teach that God's will is as narrow as the center line on the highway. If you cross it, you are out of His will. What do you teach?

A. I believe it is as wide as the road itself. It is so wide that there is room for God to change His mind:

> *"Remember Abraham, Isaac, and Israel, thy servants, to whom you swore by your own self, and said unto them, I will multiply your seed as the stars of heaven, and all this land that I have spoken of will I give unto your seed, and they shall inherit it forever. And the LORD repented of the evil which he thought to do unto his people."* (Exodus 32:13-14)

It is also flexible enough to include your will, as long as you abide in Him.

> *"If you abide in Me, and My words abide in you, you will ask what you desire, and it shall be done for you. By this My Father is glorified, that you bear much fruit; so you will be My disciples."* (John 15:7-8)

Q. You teach about fighting for the will of God. Isn't my having faith enough?

A. It does take faith, which we will need as we endure to come into the will of God and receive His promises:

> *For you have need of endurance, so that after you have done the will of God, you may receive the promise: For yet a little while, and He who is coming will come and will not tarry.* (Hebrews 10:36-37)

THE SHOTGUN PRAYER

It is amusing to listen to us charismatics praying for someone to be healed. Rather than praying by the Spirit, we pray a burst of everything we know to pray. I call it the shotgun effect, praying everything we have ever heard prayed, hoping something might hit. It goes like this:

> I have authority over you. I curse this thing. I cast Satan oooooouuuuttt! Who has some oil? I bind you, and I loose healing. I curse every generational curse. Somebody get me some oil! I perceive that you have been rejected in the past. Be blessed now! Let's lay hands on him. I declare it done! Everyone stomp on the devil's neck. Shout for joy, clap your hands. It will give us the victory! We are in agreement, aren't we, brother? Go sickness! I command it! Come on, everyone gather around. Let's all pray at once! Devil, take your hands off God's property! Who's got a handkerchief that we can pray for and send home with this brother? Be healed! Did someone go to find oil? You are healed according to His Word now accept it!

We do all this because we don't know what to do. Wouldn't it be simpler to step back and ask Jesus what He wants to do and await His instructions? When we pray our own way, we are being presumptuous. Being presumptuous means to "take too much to oneself . . . or taking the authority that belongs to another." We cannot heal at will, or we would heal everyone all the time. This would reduce the number of conversions to Christ, not increase it.

Q. Should we actually pray for God's will concerning things like buying the right car, or should we just use common sense, or just go get what we want?

A. I think we should use both; when I have acknowledged Him in all my ways, it makes buying a car a lot less stressful. I have prayed about which car to buy many times. One time, I had become aware within me of a desire to find a car that was trip-worthy for me and my young family. The car I had was all right, but it was a compact car and not designed for long-distance travel. I had an inner urge to start praying for a different car. I did this for a while, but nothing happened. So, I began going to car dealerships to look around, but I had very little money to work with. I roamed a couple of car lots, but nothing happened.

Then one day, as I was talking to a salesman, praying within for God's direction, a car seemed to stand out from all the rest. I don't want to be super-spiritual about it, but it seemed to glow, at least in my mind's eye. It was on the far side of the lot, so I pointed it out to the salesman and asked him about it. He said he didn't know anything about it because it had just come the day before on a trade-in. Somehow, I knew it was the car for me. He went to make some inquires, came back with a price I could live with, and I drove the car home.

As it turned out, right after this I began to commute from Ontario to New York to go to Bible school. Our little Ford Pinto would not have survived all that travel, but this car was perfect for it, both because it was economical on gas during the gas crisis, and it was a solid workhorse, perfect for long trips. I felt I was in the will of God.

It was Jesus who told us that we were to pray daily for God's will in heaven to be done on Earth (see Matthew 6:9-13). What if His will is actually written in books that are kept in heaven? If this is true, shouldn't we pray that His will be done on a daily basis, just as we would for our daily bread and daily forgiveness, inviting Him into all of our circumstances and into all of our decisions, so we can see more of His will manifested in our lives?

It must make God scratch His head when He sees us making our own plans, doing whatever we want to do, spending as little time in prayer as possible, just long enough to ask Him to bless our plans rather than asking Him to show us His.

PREJUDICED AGAINST THE WILL OF GOD

Q. I have learned not to say I don't like certain places because that's likely where God will send me. Why do you suppose He does that?

A. I suspect the enemy knows something of the future, maybe not completely, but he must be able to figure some things out. The reason I say this is because I have found several times where I get strong attitudes, almost a prejudice against certain places or things, only to find out later that it was the will of God for me. Here is an example.

One time my father-in-law came to our place with an envelope full of cash and a newspaper where he had circled houses for sale. He explained that he was giving Heather her inheritance then, with the idea that we should buy our first house instead of paying rent. The envelope contained enough for a downpayment, but even with that, our limited income required that we trust the Lord to find just the right place.

I arranged for a real estate agent to begin taking me around the city after work. I was not sure what to look for, but I had stipulated up front that there were two things I categorically never wanted. One was to live in the nearby town of Trenton and the second was that I would never live in a duplex, which to me meant sharing a house with someone. Every day after work, I looked at houses but came up empty. This went on for a few months, which seemed odd to me because we had a clear sense of direction that we were to get a house, but for the life of me I could not find one. Finally, I got quiet and began to seek the Lord. I asked Him to tell me plainly what I was doing wrong. He spoke to my heart right away, saying, "Look for a duplex in Trenton."

This floored me!

After humbling myself before the Lord, I found a newspaper that listed houses for sale in Trenton. There was a duplex for sale in our price range. I went to see it and knew right away it was the house for us. It turned out to be a lovely place for our young family, and we liked the neighbors, including those who lived on the other side of the duplex. Years later, when it was time to sell that house, it had tripled in value, only because of the location it was in.

Now, whenever I have a strong bias against things, or an aversion to something, it makes me wonder why, causing me to take a second look at what might be trying to block the will of God in some area of my life. This has happened to me about certain people, places, and things. I am no longer surprised that it happens, but I now understand what good things I would otherwise forfeit by not taking time to look a little closer at it.

GOD'S WILL AND DIFFICULTY

Q. You say that there is suffering while being in God's will. Doesn't hardship and suffering come to us because of the bad choices and decisions we have made?

A. There are some verses that connect the will of God to hardship and suffering:

For it is better, if it is the will of God, to suffer for doing good than for doing evil. (1 Peter 3:17)

Therefore, since Christ suffered for us in the flesh, arm yourselves also with the same mind, for he who has suffered in the flesh has ceased from sin, that he no longer should live the rest of his time in the flesh for the lusts of men, but for the will of God. (4:1-2)

Therefore let those who suffer according to the will of God commit their souls to Him in doing good, as to a faithful Creator. (v. 19)

However, I often hear people consoling themselves that they must have been in God's will because they learned so much during their times of trouble. It's not necessarily a matter of the will of God in such cases. Remember, it's God's desire that we learn and grow from all of our circumstances. Don't take the fact that you gained something from it as a confirmation of His will; take it as a consolation. We serve a God who is able to make all things work together for our good, even our wrong choices!

We see this in the story of Abraham, who went down into Egypt without consulting the Lord. He left the land of promise and almost lost his wife and his life, before going full circle and ending up back in Bethel. God used this side journey to fulfill an earlier promise He had made to Abraham. God promised that He would make Abraham rich. Before Abraham returned home, the king of Egypt gave him oxen, donkeys, sheep and goats, silver, gold, and male and female servants, which enriched Abraham's life, even though he had not been led there by the Lord. God is just that good! Amen! (See Genesis 12:10-20; 13:1-4.)

HOW VISION COMES

Q. When you talk about vision, what do you mean?

A. Not necessarily. I believe that as we seek the Lord in our prayer closets, He will begin to give us vision in the following ways:

1. **From the Scriptures:** The Bible itself is God's revealed will and purpose for mankind in a general way, but He also has a specific purpose for each person. That specific purpose should never contradict what is written in God's Word.

2. **Observing others:** We can get vision by reading books or studying the lives of others.

3. **Personal prophecy:** God can communicate vision this way, but usually it confirms what He has already been revealing to our hearts.

4. **Seeing the need:** Often, vision is released after we see a need and consider ways to meet it.

5. **Heavenly vision:** This can come from actual spiritual visions or dreams, but this is rare. It did happen several times in the apostle Paul's life.

WHAT IF HE DOES NOT RESPOND?

Q. I try to hear from the Lord, asking Him questions, but it does not seem like He responds. Why might this be?

A. We can begin by asking Him why He is not speaking. There may be a number of reasons why He is not responding. It could be anything from our level of expectation to His not being willing to compete with all the noise in our lives. If the television is always on and the music is always blaring, or we are always playing with our phone whenever there is a quiet moment, we may not hear Him at all. If while in prayer we are doing all the talking and never being still, this could also account for it. Here are some other reasons:

- **We are not taking time to learn to hear His voice:** Jesus said, *"My Sheep hear my voice."* You have to drive a deep stake into this and expect Him to speak to you just because you are His sheep. There is no shortcut to learning His voice. It takes time, proximity, and practice.

- **We are not asking Him questions:** *"You do not have because you do not ask"* (James 4:2). Notice how the disciples often asked Him questions, and He never failed to answer them. (This would make a good study for you to build your confidence in asking Him questions) Jesus rarely offered them any revelation without being asked.

Jesus is not like us in that He is not always talking for no reason.

- **He does not grace selfishness:** James went on to say in verse 3 of the fourth chapter that, when we ask, we ask amiss or for the wrong reasons: *"You do not have because you do not ask. You ask and do not receive, because you ask amiss, that you may spend it on your pleasures."*

- **We are double-minded:** James 1:8 and 4:8 describe the block of double-mindedness which occurs whenever we think about what other people think more than we think about what God thinks.

- **We need to mend broken relationships:** We cannot treat God's children like trash and then expect Him to talk with us as if nothing is wrong with that. We need to make things right, *"As far as it is within you be at peace with all men"* (Hebrews 12:14).

- **We are not quieting ourselves before Him:** We need to learn to listen. Even though David was a great leader, he learned to quiet himself like a little baby:

    Lord, my heart is not haughty, nor my eyes lofty. Neither do I concern myself with great matters, nor with things too profound for me. Surely I have calmed and quieted my soul, like a weaned child with his mother; like a weaned child is my soul within me. (Psalm 131:1-2)

- **We are not waiting with expectation:** Sometimes, our minds our too busy, too easily distracted, and not expecting much from the Lord. David said that his expectation came from the Lord: *"My soul, wait silently for God alone, for my expectation is from Him"* (Psalm 62:5).

- **We have not learned to linger:** It is important to shut out the noise and to linger in His presence. Joshua did this in Exodus 33:11, and it led to him coming into his ministry. We need to truly believe that Jesus is as real today as He was two thousand years ago. If we spend time with Him, we will hear Him. That is a fact.

- **We are disobeying Him:** When we have spurned what He has already said, why would He speak again? Saul had ignored the Lord's voice in the past and did what he wanted to do instead (see 1 Samuel 15:1-35; 28:5-6). Then when Saul asked Him questions, God ignored him. If we continue to disobey what He has clearly said, both to our hearts and in His written Word, He will not speak to us.

- **We are doing your own thing:** There is something called "lawlessness," which means we want to do our own thing. (It would be good to do a word study of this to see how serious it is.) You cannot have it both ways; it's either your way or His way.

- **We are proud:** God still resists the proud (see James 4:6; 1 Peter 5:5). Resisting is the feeling you get when you try to push two magnets together from the opposite sides. When He has resisted me, I do not hear from Him. When this happens, it's time to get honest before Him, especially about my true motives.

- **We are presumptuous:** Check to see if there are major areas of your life where you pushed your way into something that may not have been the will of God. Saul was also presumptuous, having a bigger view of himself than he should have. It caused the Lord to resist him and to refuse to answer Saul when Saul inquired of Him.

- **We have made light of His counsel in the past:** There is a powerful section of Proverbs 1:22-33, where Wisdom asks us:

How long, you simple ones, will you love simplicity? For scorners delight in their scorning, and fools hate knowledge. Turn at my rebuke; surely I will pour out my spirit on you; I will make my words known to you. Because I have called and you refused, I have stretched out my hand and no one regarded, because you disdained all my counsel, and would have none of my rebuke, I also will laugh at your calamity; I will mock when your terror comes, when your terror comes like a storm, and your destruction comes like a whirlwind, when distress and anguish come upon you. Then they will call on me, but I will not answer; they will seek me diligently, but they will not find me. Because they hated knowledge and did not choose the fear of the Lord, they would have none of my counsel and despised my every rebuke. Therefore they shall eat the fruit of their own way, and be filled to the full with their own fancies. For the turning away of the simple will slay them, and the complacency of fools will destroy them; but whoever listens to me will dwell safely, and will be secure, without fear of evil.

- **We are not treating our wives properly:** In 1 Peter 3:7, husbands are warned about how they treat their wives: *"Husbands, likewise, dwell with them with understanding, giving honor to the wife, as to the weaker vessel, and as being heirs together of the grace of life, that your prayers may not be hindered."*

We must treat our wives as Christians, which is something we tend forget. As I studied this verse, it seems that God has built in a special protection for wives to prevent them from being mistreated by their authority. He decided that He would refuse their husbands' prayers, which would affect their husbands means of provision, protection, and guidance. In my own experience, when I have not treated my wife properly, I have found that my prayers seem to only hit the ceiling and never leave the room. They are totally ineffective, and my desire to pray is greatly diminished.

Q. How can I know for sure God is speaking?

A. You may not know 100 percent. This is all by faith, but we need to believe the Bible, which says, that God is always speaking in some way or other: *"For God does speak, now one way, now another, though man may not perceive it."* (Job 33:14)

I have learned that it does not all depend upon my great ability to hear as much as it depends upon His great ability to speak.

Here are some ways that God speaks to us and some of the means He uses:

- His written Word
- An inner voice
- The inner witness of the Spirit
- Inspired thought or impressions
- Our conscience
- Mental pictures
- His peace
- Wisdom and common sense
- Our physical senses
- Nature
- The counsel of other people
- Prophecy
- Angels
- World events
- Coincidences
- Circumstances
- An audible voice
- Visions
- Dreams

THE PURPOSE OF DREAMS

Q. Why is there so little teaching about dreams?

A. I believe it is because these dreams, visions, visitations of angels, and the hearing of an audible voice are less frequently used methods of guidance. All are biblical, but they are also very rare. I am wary of those who experience them too often. Also, I would discount it if they were too casual about this form of guidance. When God gave visions or dreams to people in the Bible, they often became completely "unglued" because of the fear of the Lord that accompanied these experiences. A bona-fide prophet may experience more of these as a part of their ministry, but the rest of us do not. If someone is seeing visions all the time or dreaming prophetically on a regular basis, I would be reluctant to receive it as from the Lord. The same is true concerning those who have personal words from the Lord all the time. As I survey the Scriptures and look back at my own history, I would say the Lord does not speak to us in this way as often as some would have us believe.

The Lord made a distinction between visions and dreams when He prophesied through Joel that in the last days, old men would dream dreams and young men would see visions (see Joel 2:28).

I am sure there are other ways of interpreting this verse, but one way that I think of old men seeing dreams is that they perceive the purposes of God for the next generation, seeing things that they themselves will not participate in. They see such things with spiritual longing, but others will fulfill those things. Young men, on the other hand, with years ahead of them tend to see visions that involve themselves.

Not all dreams are from the Lord. Some simply reveal what has been trapped in our minds during the day, what we have been meditating on. They are just below our awareness level and tend to surface when our guard is down. For most people, this happens just before they sleep or just before they awaken.

I do, however, believe that God uses dreams to speak to us. I have experienced it a couple of times myself. One of the reasons He does this is because we are not open to His correction, so He speaks in a way we can hear. We can see this in the following verse, where the wise man says, *"He opens the ears of men, and seals their instruction."* The word *instruction* here can mean *correction*.

"In a dream, in a vision of the night, when deep sleep falls upon men, while slumbering on their beds, then He opens the ears of men, and seals their instruction. In order to turn man from his deed, and conceal pride from man, He keeps back his soul from the Pit, and his life from perishing by the sword." (Job 33:15-18)

DREAMS OFTEN CONTAIN WARNINGS

Another reason God speaks to us in dreams is to warn us of things to come. Here are some biblical examples of this:

- God warned Abimelech of the punishment pending for taking Sarah (see Genesis 20:3-7).

- God warned Laban about taking advantage of or hurting Jacob (see Genesis 31:10-11; 24-25).

- God warned Joseph not to reject Mary (see Matthew 1:20-21).

- God warned the wise men about Herod (see Matthew 2:12-13).

- God told Joseph to return to Israel but warned him about where to live (see Matthew 2:19-23).

- God showed Pilate's wife what they were doing was wrong (see Matthew 27:19)

- God also gives us dreams to warn us or prepare us for the future (see Genesis 37:5-9; Daniel 4:5-10).

Sometimes, dreams reveal both good and bad aspects of our future (see Genesis 40:5-8; Genesis 41:1-8) Sometimes dreams contain confirmation, like they did in Gideon's situation (see Judges 7:13-14).

And, sometimes, God reveals Himself to us in dreams (see Numbers 12:6-8; 1 Kings 3:5).

I do not believe God speaks to us in riddles or dark sayings anymore. Some dreams are just plain weird. I don't think these are the Holy Spirit speaking because dreams should contain revelation if they are from Him:

But now, brethren, if I come to you speaking with tongues, what shall I profit you unless I speak to you either by revelation, by knowledge, by prophesying, or by teaching? (1 Corinthians 14:6)

NEGATIVE FORMS OF FINDING GUIDANCE

Do not inquire about the future by fortunetellers, horoscopes, or mediums. We should never accept guidance by the reading of palms, cards, crystal balls, or Ouija Boards. We should not read other people's minds. God's Word forbids that we use fortunetellers, go to séances, or use any other evil method of foretelling. These are the enemy's counterfeit methods of guidance. If you do this, demons will become an unwelcome part of your life.

Finally, don't over-spiritualize your spiritual life. In reality, the more spiritual you become, the more practical your life will be.

BECOME A PATHFINDER

Q. What is one of the best ways to grow in my ability to be guided by the Lord?

A. Become a pathfinder. A pathfinder is a military name given to a soldier who is specially trained to operate navigational equipment in order to guide the main airborne body to the drop zones.

Pathfinder teams are dropped ahead of the main body in order to locate designated drop zones and provide radio and visual guides for the main force to improve the accuracy of the jump.

In terms of this Study Guide, this material has been accumulated through the years from what I learned as I have helped guide others into the will of God. The goal is for you to become a pathfinder, doing the same thing. I have listed some guidelines about guidance which have helped me along the way. As you know, guidance does not come automatically; it is a skill that must be learned, often through trial and error. It also comes as we cultivate an intimate relationship with the Guide, who wants to be the Lord of our lives continually, not just when we need something. The Lord does not want to be a "guidance dispenser."

SOWING IN PRAYER

Q. You use the term *sowing in prayer*. Can you give me an example of this from your life?

A. For a long while, I felt bored out of my skull. I had pastored a church from the earliest phases of growth and had spent all my "firsts," which meant by now I had done all the new and exciting things and now the prospect in front of me was merely maintaining. I loved my church and was surrounded by loving and supportive people, but I felt hemmed in. I wanted more, more of whatever, but did not have the wherewithal to get there. I felt like I had plateaued early and I was clearly discontent. I knew it was not healthy to stay in this condition, so I began to seek the Lord. It was only then that I could get down to the real issues of my heart.

I finally sorted it out in prayer, and it came down to this: I was bored with church and with my level of Christian experience, but I was not bored with the Lord. In fact, I wanted more of Him. I realized that I was hungry for Him and His power in my life. I wanted to see more of Him at work, not church politics as usual. I began crying out for more, keeping it before Him, praying again and again. I didn't do this out of fear that He would not do it, but more for my own sake, to keep me focused. My main prayer was, "Lord, take me some place where I do not know anyone. Take me someplace where they don't take Visa, where I have to trust You, to see more of Your power at work in my life. Take me someplace where You and I can work together. I want to see Your power!"

I had prayed this way for about two years. Nothing had changed circumstantially, yet I was more expectant and excited than ever. I was wondering how He was going to do it, where it would lead, and how it would change my life. It was during this timeframe that the Lord awakened my heart to the poor, doing something more than giving money to them. He birthed the message of "Incarnation" in me. I felt like I was being brought into something, a whole new level, but I did not know what that would look like in my everyday life. I just knew I did not want to die in the pew. I had read about lots of ways Christians had died—by shipwreck, by disease while caring for the lost, by sword. The worst death I could think of would be "death by pew," and I kept praying, "Lord, don't leave me here. Don't leave me in this condition. Take me somewhere. Take me by the heart and lead me!"

It was after this time of seeking the Lord that I was invited to go to a remote jungle region in Northern India to work with a small group of Christians who were trying to reach a primitive tribe for Christ. God didn't just open the door to a new geographic location on the globe, but He gave me a new heart in the process. The process was everything. I shudder to think what would have happened had I not sought the Lord.

TIMING IS EVERYTHING

Q. I seem to hear from the Lord but often get the timing wrong. Can you speak to this?

A. The timing aspect of guidance is always the most difficult part, even for the most seasoned seeker. Moses knew he was called to deliver Israel, and even saw their need as he walked around Egypt. He tried to intervene in his own strength, but he was forty years too early.

> *"Now when he was forty years old, it came into his heart to visit his brethren, the children of Israel. And seeing one of them suffer wrong, he defended and avenged him who was oppressed, and struck down the Egyptian. For he supposed that his brethren would have understood that God would deliver them by his hand, but they did not understand."* (Acts 7:23-25)

Saul was a young man when he received a vision about his purpose on the road to Damascus. The Lord revealed to him that he would stand before kings and give his testimony. We know that the book of Acts spans about a thirty-year period, but it is not until the end of Paul's ministry when he was an old man that we read about him standing before kings (see Acts 9:15; 26:1-23). Even then, the route Paul was taken that eventually led to a place where he could preach before kings would likely have been so different than what he had imagined. He testified before kings in chains.

Joseph is another great example of someone who was shown part of his future in a dream when he was just a boy, a vision of greatness, but the route to fulfillment was so different from what he could have imagined. The doors God eventually opened to him to become the second highest person in all the earth were doors that led to a well, an auction block, and a prison. The way up was down.

Perhaps the most striking example of someone who was far different from what was shown about him in a vision was Aaron. Moses had received a vision about what the high priest would look like and what he would do. The vision is almost a chapter long, detailing all the clothes Aaron would wear. Then, suddenly, God breaks off from this vision and tells Moses to get down off the mountain because there was trouble in the camp. Moses goes down to where the Children of Israel are camped, only to find Aaron leading them in a naked parade before a golden calf. At that very moment, Aaron was a long way from how God saw him on the mountain.

There is usually a gap between what God says about us and what we are really capable of. It is in this gap that He plans to transform us to become what He saw in our potential. I actually pity those who overrun this gap, thinking they are what He revealed about them, without waiting upon Him to bring it to pass. They are often the ones we see who have gifts and potential but without the character. Remember, He is the God who calls those things that be not as though they were.

IN THE FULLNESS OF TIME

There is a little phrase often used in the Bible; *"in the fullness of time."* We have to wait for the fullness of time. An example of this is when people were praying for the angry young Pharisee named Saul of Tarsus, who was bent on destroying the church and wreaking havoc in people's lives. They must have prayed for him to come to know the Lord. Later Saul, now named Paul, wrote that he came to Jesus in the fullness of time:

> *But when it pleased God, who separated me from my mother's womb, and called me by his grace, to reveal his Son in me, that I might preach him among the heathen; immediately I conferred not with flesh and blood: Neither went I up to Jerusalem to them which were apostles before me; but I went into Arabia.* (Galatians 1:15-17)

Time is in the Father's hands, and He does not always show us too much in advance.

WANTING IT SO BAD YOU ARE WILLING TO WAIT

Be especially careful when you want something so bad you are not willing to wait for it to come to pass or to let God bring it to you. God almost always delays His answers, yet somehow, they are always on time. He does this to be gracious to us and to be glorified. In the end, all we can do is worship Him: *"Therefore the Lord will wait, that He may be gracious to you; and therefore He will be exalted, that He may have mercy on you"* (Isaiah 30:18). You know you have come into the right kind of thinking about waiting when you find yourself praying, "Lord, I want this so bad that I will wait for it."

To read more about waiting upon the will of God, see my book, *The Work of Waiting*.

THE RIGHT VISION, BUT THE WRONG TIME

I always felt that I was to write and produce books and other printed material. When a friend of mine told me that he was getting rid of his printing press, I asked him for it. He gave it to me freely, along with all the equipment needed to begin printing books. When I told a man in our church about it, he offered to run the press for me, all for no charge. Then things began to snowball quickly.

As other equipment became available, some free, others at a low cost, it looked like the provision of the Lord. The final thing was a building to house it all, which came my way in the form of a construction modular, a trailer, worth thousands of dollars. It was given to me, along with the land and free-electrical hook-up to boot. The timing of all this seemed perfect.

We set up shop in less time than it takes to tell about it. When other people saw what was happening, they came forward, offering their skills to help. Beyond this, one of the local paper mills agreed to give us all the paper we wanted—free. Soon, tons began to arrive at our little trailer, but it had to be managed right away. This meant cutting it down to a manageable size and storing it properly. If we didn't do this and moisture got to it, the ink would not adhere. This meant lots of cutting had to be done, all by hand. We had done some printing, which turned out to be more time-consuming than any of us had ever expected. We had to overcome many obstacles, all of which took time and attention. We thought the devil was trying to keep us from doing the will of God, so we worked even harder, but soon began to run out of steam. Vision will only carry you so far.

As it began to unravel, the printer got a new job, making it impossible for him to continue. Others who had said they would help were not as available anymore. Then, the free electricity came to an end, and we were spending more money than we were taking in. A local building inspector happened to see the trailer and stopped in to tell us that our building was not up to code, and to comply, it would be very costly.

Then, late one night, as I stood at a machine cutting paper, I happened to look out the trailer door that had been propped open to let the cool night air in, and I saw Jesus with the eyes of my heart, standing outside the trailer looking in. He was mostly obscured by the night and was standing at a distance from me. Somehow, I knew He was crying. He didn't say anything, but I knew what I was doing deeply grieved Him. The thought occurred to me that I had undergone years of rigorous training and preparing for ministry. I was called and equipped by Jesus to serve Him, but now was spending all my time managing paper. I dropped to my knees.

That night I repented for being out of His will. In an instant, I saw the pride of my heart. I knew I would have to humble myself before those who had been involved with the project, telling each one how I had missed it, which I did. Everyone was very gracious to me and shared their own misgivings that they had felt from the start. I asked the Lord to help me dispose of everything, which He did with astounding speed. We learned that a Bible school needed printing equipment, so we gave it to them. They trucked it away, and I could not have been happier. In the middle of all this, a local printer with whom I had done some business came to me and offered the complete use of his building and equipment. They would do the printing for me as time permitted. He gave me the keys to his building—all for free.

As I look back on all of this, many years later, I can see how the vision for publishing was from the Lord, but I was way too early. When the vision finally did come about, others had approached me, telling me it was time to do it, and there was an amazing convergence of resources that made it burden free.

KNOWING HIS KNOCK

The Bible says Jesus is knocking at our heart's door. What does this sound like? How does it feel? How can we discern His knocking? I asked the Lord this once, as I was not sure I was able to hear it. He helped me to see that it could be different for every person, but that I would begin to know it. The next morning, I felt His knock, which came in the form of a desire or prompting to meet Him in prayer. As I acted upon it, I began to notice that it happened more and more. After this, I could honestly say that I knew His knock.

It is my hope and desire that these notes may help you will begin to know His voice and His knock so that your fellowship with Him will grow.

REFERENCE NOTES

1. *Crucial Experiences in the Life of D.L. Moody* by Paul Gericke, as mentioned in an article posted on *Christianity Today* https://www.christianitytoday.com/history/issues/issue-25/world-has-yet-to-see.html

2. Jim Elliot: Jim Elliot Quotes. (n.d.). BrainyQuote.com. Retrieved September 12, 2020, from BrainyQuote.com Web site: https://www.brainyquote.com/quotes/jim_elliot_189251

3. http://www.canadahistory.com/sections/eras/2%20worlds%20meet/Frobisher.html

4. Jim Elliot: Jim Elliot Quotes. (n.d.). BrainyQuote.com. Retrieved September 12, 2020, from BrainyQuote.com Web site: https://www.brainyquote.com/quotes/jim_elliot_189251

5. "Sweet Surrender" lyrics by John Denver © BMG Rights Management US, LLC, Walt Disney Music Company.

6. Here is a link that tells the story of how they worked out the voice of God: https://www.imdforums.com/threads/the-prince-of-egypt-1998.5193/

ADDENDUM ONE: PRAYERS AND PROMISES FOR GUIDANCE

Here is a study where the word *guide* has been taken from Scripture from a variety of translations and where it has been used in prayers and promises for those who were seeking guidance:

Abraham's servant prayed as he was sent to find a bride for Isaac:

"So this afternoon when I came to the spring I prayed this prayer: 'O Lord, the God of my master, Abraham, if you are planning to make my mission a success, please guide me in a special way.'" (Genesis 24:42 NLT)

Moses prayed:

"With unfailing love you will lead this people whom you have ransomed. You will guide them in your strength to the place where your holiness dwells." (Exodus 15:13 NLT)

"In your unfailing love you will lead the people you have redeemed. In your strength you will guide them to your holy dwelling." (Exodus 15:13 NIV)

Be my guide, O Lord, in the ways of your righteousness, because of those who are against me; make your way straight before my face. (Psalm 5:8 BBE)

He makes a resting-place for me in the green fields: he is my guide by the quiet waters. (23:2 BBE)

He gives new life to my soul: he is my guide in the ways of righteousness because of his name. (v. 3 BBE)

Be my guide and teacher in the true way; for you are the God of my salvation; I am waiting for your word all the day. (Psalm 25:5 BBE)

You are my refuge and defense; guide me and lead me as you have promised. (31:3 GNT)

Lord, teach me your ways, and guide me to do what is right because I have enemies. (27:11 NCV)

With your advice you guide me, and in the end you will take me to glory. (73:24 GWT)

You will guide me with Your counsel, and afterward receive me to glory. (v. 24)

Sustain me, my God, according to your promise, and I will live; do not let my hopes be dashed. (Psalm 119:116 NIV)

Guide my steps as you promised; don't let any sin control me. (v. 133 NCV)

You are my God; teach me to do your will. Be good to me, and guide me on a safe path. (143:10 GNTA)

Teach me to do what pleases you, because you are my God. Guide me by your good spirit into good land. (143:10 CEV)

Your hand would always be there to guide me. Your right hand would still be holding me close. (169:10 NIrV)

"Lord, you are honest and fair. You guide those who do what is right. You lead them on a straight path. You make their way smooth." (Isaiah 26:7 NIrV)

Here are promises:

Now the Lord said to Abram, "Go out from your country and from your family and from your father's house, into the land to which I will be your guide." (Genesis 12:1 BBE)

"And I will be your guide into the land which I made an oath to give to Abraham, to Isaac, and to Jacob; and I will give it to you for your heritage: I am Yahweh." (Exodus 6:8 BBE)

"God went ahead of them in a Pillar of Cloud during the day to guide them on the way, and at night in a Pillar of Fire to give them light; thus they could travel both day and night." (13:21 MSG)

"See, I am sending an angel before you, to keep you on your way and to be your guide into the place which I have made ready for you." (23:20 BBE)

"I will send an angel to guide you, and I will drive out the Canaanites, the Amorites, the Hittites, the Perizzites, the Hivites, and the Jebusites." (33:2 GNT)

"Now go, lead the people to the place I told you about. Remember that my angel will guide you, but the time is coming when I will punish these people for their sin." (32:34 GNT)

I will instruct you and teach you in the way you should go; I will guide you with My eye. Do not be like the horse or like the mule, which have no understanding, Which must be harnessed with bit and bridle, Else they will not come near you. (Psalm 32:8-9)

"I will instruct thee and teach thee in the way which thou shalt go: I will guide thee with mine eye." (32:8 KJV)

The Lord says, "I will guide you along the best pathway for your life. I will advise you and watch over you." (32:8 NLT)

For this is God, our God forever and ever; He will be our guide even to death. (48:14)

"I guide you in the way of wisdom and lead you along straight paths." (Proverbs 4:11 NIV)

"If you start to deviate from the path, you will have a voice that corrects you and guides you back to the path." (Isaiah 30:21 paraphrased)

"For I hold you by your right hand—I, the Lord your God. And I say to you, 'Don't be afraid. I am here to help you.'" (41:13 TLB)

"For you shall not go out with haste, nor go by flight; For the Lord will go before you, and the God of Israel will be your rear guard." (52:12)

"For you shall go out with joy, and be led out with peace; the mountains and the hills shall break forth into singing before you, and all the trees of the field shall clap their hands." (55:12)

"The Lord will guide you continually, and satisfy your soul in drought, and strengthen your bones; You shall be like a watered garden, and like a spring of water, whose waters do not fail." (58:11)

"And the Lord will be your guide at all times; in dry places he will give you water in full measure, and will make strong your bones; and you will be like a watered garden, and like an ever-flowing spring." (58:11 BBE)

"The Lord will guide you continually and provide for you, even in parched places. He will rescue your bones. You will be like a watered garden, like a spring of water that won't run dry." (58:11 CEV)

"Will you not from this time cry to Me, 'My father, You are the guide of my youth?'" (Jeremiah 3:4)

"Will you not from this time cry to me, My Father, you are the guide of my youth? (3:4 WEB)

"And I will give you leaders after my own heart, who will guide you with knowledge and understanding." (v. 15 NLT)

The Lord is good to those who wait for Him, to the soul who seeks Him. (Lamentations 3:25)

"To give light to those who sit in darkness and the shadow of death, to guide our feet into the way of peace." (Luke 1:79)

"Howbeit when he, the Spirit of truth, is come, he shall guide you into all the truth: for he shall not speak from himself; but what things soever he shall hear, [these] shall he speak: and he shall declare unto you the things that are to come." (John 16:13 ASV)

ADDENDUM TWO: PROMISES THAT BUILD ASSURANCE

- **A promise for those who seek Him with their whole desire:**

And all Judah rejoiced at the oath: for they had sworn with all their heart, and sought him with their whole desire; and he was found of them: and the Lord gave them rest round about. (2 Chronicles 15:15)

- **A promise of success to those who seek God in all they do:**

And in every work that he began in the service of the house of God, and in the law, and in the commandments, to seek his God, he did it with all his heart, and prospered. (2 Chronicles 31:21)

- **A promise of effectiveness for young people who are trying to seek the Lord:**

For in the eighth year of his reign, [Josiah] while he was yet young, he began to seek after the God of David his father: and in the twelfth year he began to purge Judah and Jerusalem from the high places, and the groves, and the carved images, and the molten images. (2 Chronicles 34:3)

- **Asa sought the Lord and prospered:**

Asa did what was good and right in the eyes of the Lord his God, for he removed the altars of the foreign gods and the high places, and broke down the sacred pillars and cut down the wooden images. He commanded Judah to seek the Lord God of their fathers, and to observe the law and the commandment. He also removed the high places and the incense altars from all the cities of Judah, and the kingdom was quiet under him. And he built fortified cities in Judah, for the land had rest; he had no war in those years, because the Lord had given him rest. Therefore he said to Judah, "Let us build these cities and make walls around them, and towers, gates, and bars, while the land is yet before us, because we have sought the Lord our God; we have sought Him, and He has given us rest on every side." So they built and prospered. (2 Chronicles 14:2-7)

- **As long as he sought the Lord he prospered:**

"Uzziah was sixteen years old when he became king, and he reigned fifty-two years in Jerusalem. His mother's name was Jecholiah of Jerusalem. And he did what was right in the sight of the Lord, according to all that his father Amaziah had done. He sought God in the days of Zechariah, who had understanding in the visions of God; and as long as he sought the Lord, God made him prosper." (2 Chronicles 26:3-5)

- **A promise that God will motivate you to speak and teach:**

  For Ezra had prepared his heart to seek the law of the Lord, and to do it, and to teach in Israel statutes and judgments. (Ezra 7:10)

- **There are pastors who refuse to seek the Lord:**

  "For the shepherds have become dull-hearted, and have not sought the Lord; therefore they shall not prosper, and all their flocks shall be scattered." (Jeremiah 10:21)

- **A promise for those who call upon God in difficult circumstances:**

  Moreover the word of the Lord came to Jeremiah a second time, while he was still shut up in the court of the prison, saying, "Thus says the Lord who made it, the Lord who formed it to establish it (the Lord is His name): Call to Me, and I will answer you, and show you great and mighty things, which you do not know." (Jeremiah 33:1-3)

ADDENDUM THREE: PROMISES AND PRINCIPLES OF GUIDANCE

The following verses contain the word *guide* which can be mined for promises and principles in guidance:

- **God may not guide you via the easiest route or the most logical way:**

    After Pharaoh had let the people go, God did not guide them to the highway that goes through the land of the P'lishtim, because it was close by—God thought that the people, upon seeing war, might change their minds and return to Egypt. (Exodus 13:17 CJB)

- **We should never want to "go it alone":**

    And Moses said to the Lord, See, you say to me, "Be this people's guide on their journey," but you have not made clear to me whom you will send with me. But you have said, "I have knowledge of you by name, and you have grace in my eyes." (Exodus 33:12 BBE)

- **When He guides us, there may be risks and hardships:**

    "Who was your guide through that great and cruel waste, where there were poison-snakes and scorpions and a dry land without water; who made water come out of the hard rock for you." (Deuteronomy 8:15 BBE)

- **Looking back, we will always see His faithfulness:**

    "And he has been our guide to this place, and has given us this land, a land flowing with milk and honey." (Deuteronomy 26:9 BBE)

- **He will guide us in such a way that we will not need much:**

    "For forty years I have been your guide through the waste land: your clothing has not become old on your backs, or your shoes on your feet." (Deuteronomy 29:5 BBE)

- **He will show us that He is all we really need:**

    So the Lord only was his guide, no other god was with him. (Deuteronomy 32:12 BBE)

- **He will guide us from our youth:**

    Then David the king went in and took his seat before the Lord, and said, "Who am I, O Lord God, and what is my family, that you have been my guide till now?" (2 Samuel 7:18 BBE)

- **To always be in need of the Lord is a sign of strength, not of weakness:**

    So Jotham became strong, because in all his ways he made the Lord his guide. (2 Chronicles 27:6)

- **He will never forsake us:**

  "You, in Your great compassion, did not forsake them in the wilderness; the pillar of cloud did not leave them by day, to guide them on their way, nor the pillar of fire by night, to light for them the way in which they were to go." (Nehemiah 9:19 NAS)

- **He is a Father who provides whatever we need:**

  "For I was cared for by God as by a father from my earliest days; he was my guide from my mother's womb!" (Job 31:18)

- **Being honest through and through pays off:**

  The integrity of the upright will guide them, but the perversity of the unfaithful will destroy them. (Proverbs 11:3 NKJV)

- **The best guidance begins on the inside:**

  If your spiritual nature is your guide, you are not subject to Moses' laws. (Galatians 5:18 GW)

- **Another nature on the inside will also try to lead you:**

  When you do things, do not let selfishness or pride be your guide. Instead, be humble and give more honor to others than to yourselves. (Philippians 2:3 NCV)

- **Your flesh cannot manufacture the same kind of peace that Christ gives:**

  The peace that Christ gives is to guide you in the decisions you make; for it is to this peace that God has called you together in the one body. And be thankful. (Colossians 3:15 GNT)

ADDENDUM FOUR: BOOKS I RECOMMEND

- *Cultivating Your Call*
- *Welcome to the Wilderness*
- *The Day*
- *A Place for Prophecy*
- *The Work of Waiting*

OTHER PEOPLE'S BOOKS

- *God's Smuggler* by Brother Andrew has been one of the best books I have come across that shows how God has a specific and unique will for each person's life. This amazing story illustrates how to hear from God, grapple with guidance, and find purpose.

- *The Cross and the Switchblade* by David Wilkerson is a dynamic story filled with examples of how to seek the Lord, hear from God, and discern His will.

- *Is That Really You, God?* was written by Loren Cunningham as a way to tell the story of how Youth With A Mission (YWAM) came to be. It is masterly woven together with insightful stories that help young people learn the principles of guidance and hearing the voice of God.